ASSESSMENT OF
HUMAN CHARACTERISTICS

Arthur N. Wiens, Ph.D.
Department of Medical Psychology
University of Oregon Medical School
Portland 1, Oregon

BASIC CONCEPTS IN PSYCHOLOGY SERIES
developed at The University of Michigan
Edward L. Walker, Editor

GENERAL

PSYCHOLOGY AS A NATURAL AND SOCIAL SCIENCE	Edward L. Walker
TEACHING THE BEGINNING COURSE IN PSYCHOLOGY	Edward L. Walker and Wilbert J. McKeachie
A LABORATORY MANUAL FOR THE CONTROL AND ANALYSIS OF BEHAVIOR	Harlan L. Lane and Daryl Bem
QUANTIFICATION IN PSYCHOLOGY	William L. Hays
BASIC STATISTICS	**William L. Hays**

PSYCHOLOGY: A NATURAL SCIENCE

NEUROPSYCHOLOGY: THE STUDY OF BRAIN AND BEHAVIOR	Charles M. Butter
SENSORY PROCESSES	Mathew Alpern, Merle Lawrence, and David Wolsk
PERCEPTION	Daniel J. Weintraub and Edward L. Walker
PERCEPTUAL DEMONSTRATION KIT	Daniel J. Weintraub and Edward L. Walker
HUMAN PERFORMANCE	Paul M. Fitts **and Michael I. Posner**
CONDITIONING AND INSTRUMENTAL LEARNING	Edward L. Walker

PSYCHOLOGY: A SOCIAL SCIENCE

MOTIVATION: A STUDY OF ACTION	David Birch and Joseph Veroff
THE CONCEPT OF HUMAN DEVELOPMENT	Elton B. McNeil
PSYCHODYNAMICS: THE SCIENCE OF UNCONSCIOUS MENTAL FORCES	Gerald S. Blum
ASSESSMENT OF HUMAN CHARACTERISTICS	E. Lowell Kelly
COGNITIVE PROCESSES	Melvin Manis
SOCIAL PSYCHOLOGY: AN EXPERIMENTAL APPROACH	Robert B. Zajonc

ASSESSMENT OF HUMAN CHARACTERISTICS

E. LOWELL KELLY

The University of Michigan

BROOKS/COLE PUBLISHING COMPANY

Belmont, California

A Division of Wadsworth Publishing Company, Inc.

L.C. Cat. Card No.: 67-25823

Printed in the United States of America

SERIES FOREWORD

Basic Concepts in Psychology was conceived as a series of brief paperback volumes constituting a beginning textbook in psychology. Several unique advantages arise from publishing individual chapters as separate volumes rather than under a single cover. Each book or chapter can be written by an author identified with the subject matter of the area. New chapters can be added, individual chapters can be revised independently, and, possibly, competitive chapters can be provided for controversial areas. Finally, to a degree, an instructor of the beginning course in psychology can choose a particular set of chapters to meet the needs of his students.

Probably the most important impetus for the series came from the fact that a suitable textbook did not exist for the beginning courses in psychology at the University of Michigan—Psychology 100 (Psychology as a Natural Science) and Psychology 101 (Psychology as a Social Science). In addition, no laboratory manual treated both the natural science and social science problems encountered in the first laboratory course, Psychology 110.

For practical rather than ideological reasons, the initial complement of authors comes from the staff of the University of Michigan. Coordination among geographically dispersed authors seems needlessly difficult, and the diversity of points of view in the Department of Psychology at Michigan makes the danger of parochialism quite small.

Each author in the Basic Concepts in Psychology Series has considerable freedom. He has been charged to devote approximately half of his resources to elementary concepts and half to topics of special interest and emphasis. In this way, each volume will reflect the personality and viewpoint of the author while presenting the subject matter usually found in a chapter of an elementary textbook.

INTRODUCTION

In this small volume I have attempted to provide the reader with a broad overview of the approaches to, the methods of, and the complex problems of human assessment. As the reader will note, I feel strongly that improved assessment techniques are critically needed both in the development of the basic science of psychology and in the applied fields of industrial, clinical, counseling, and educational psychology.

As far as possible I have tried to present the material in a manner intelligible to students who have not yet had courses in statistical methods or psychological measurement. Readers interested in an introduction to statistics are referred to Hays' *Basic Statistics,* and those who want to delve further into the theory of psychological measurement are urged to read Hays' *Quantification in Psychology,* both in this series.

In writing any book an author becomes indebted to many persons who have contributed to it. I greatly appreciated the suggestions received from four colleagues who read an early draft of the manuscript — Allen L. Edwards, Bert F. Green, Jr., Alfred B. Heilbrun, and Leona E. Tyler. I also wish to thank the Series Editor, Edward L. Walker, and the copy editor, Robert Mann, for their editorial assistance; my wife Lillian for preparing the indices; my secretary, Mrs. Ferne Galantai, for translating my handwriting into a readable manuscript.

CONTENTS

ASSESSMENT OF
HUMAN CHARACTERISTICS

WHAT IS ASSESSMENT?

The term "assessment" is relatively new in psychological parlance. If the student consults a dictionary—even an unabridged one—he will discover that "assessment" is defined solely in financial terms, i.e., the apportionment of taxes (or some other financial contribution) to be collected from property owners (or members of an association) for the support of a governmental unit (or associational activities). The use of the term "assessment" by psychologists first occurred during World War II to describe the procedures used by a group of psychologists and psychiatrists to select individuals specially qualified for demanding "cloak and dagger" assignments essential to the worldwide wartime efforts of the Office of Strategic Services. The term first appeared in psychological literature in the title of the book describing this unique program of personnel selection, *The Assessment of Men* (OSS Staff, 1942). Following World War II, it was natural that the psychologists who had participated in the OSS selection program continued to use the term assessment in their teaching and research publications. In 1953, the present author was invited to prepare the first of a series of chapters for the *Annual Review of Psychology* on "The Theory and Techniques of Assessment." And more recently the term assessment has begun to appear in psychology texts—even in their titles (Vernon, 1964).

To psychologists assessment has come to mean any procedure for making meaningful evaluations or differentiations among human beings with respect to any characteristic or attribute. In common use, assessment has become a very broad term that is applied to all of the following: any judgments regarding one's fellow man; the evaluation of application forms; the writing and evaluation of letters of recommendation; the selection interview; the assignment of grades in schools and colleges; the testing of achievement, knowledge, or skills; the intensive clinical study involved in the diagnosis of an individual suffering from a mental disorder; and the use of any one of the hundreds of psychological tests which psychologists have developed to measure human abilities, aptitudes, natures, needs, attitudes, interests, and values. Thus the term includes a variety of *methods* of assessment and an even greater range of attributes or characteristics by which a person may be assesssed. Assessment is a process that goes on throughout one's life—in the home, in school, in industry and government, as well as in specialized institutions or programs. It is a process in which all of us engage, either as amateurs or professionals. And, since the accurate assessment of any characteristic is an extremely complex problem, it is hardly surprising that the quality of assessments varies from relatively good to completely worthless.

Although all members of the human race are sufficiently similar to assure their proper classification in the species *homo sapiens*, it is a fascinating fact that no two of all of the billions of persons in the world are exactly alike. Identical twins are not completely identical at birth, and further dissimilarities develop throughout the lives of each twin pair. Every individual is a unique person, with a particular constellation of attributes which makes him different from anyone else. He has an individual identity; and his identity is sufficiently important, both to him as a person and to society, that he is given a name of his own. And, because two or more individuals may be given identical names, many societies provide for more dependable identification by the assignment of numbers (e.g., a social security number).

Although individual identity is extremely important to the person, to members of his family, to his employer, to his insurance company, and, in the case of a crime, to the police, and although intensive studies of the lives of single individuals often lead to fascinating biographies, assessment psychologists focus not on the uniqueness of each individual but rather on the differences of each person *vis-à-vis* other persons, i.e., the ways in which *and* the degree to which Person A is similar to or differs from other persons.

WHY ASSESS?

THE PERVASIVENESS OF INDIVIDUAL DIFFERENCES

"In the first place, no two persons are born exactly alike, but each differs from each in natural endowments, one being suited for one occupation, and another for another." This statement from Plato's *Republic* suggests that the range of human characteristics was recognized long before the days of modern psychology. Indeed, historic recognition of individual differences is clearly shown by the thousands of words in every major language which describe persons and emphasize their salient characteristics. For example, Allport and Odbert (1936) list some 18,000 English words descriptive of persons, and even this array is not sufficient for the full verbal descriptions of individuals—for example, adjectives are often modified by an adverb like "more," "less," or "very."

SCIENTIFIC CURIOSITY AND UNDERSTANDING

Man has long been fascinated by the range of differences among his fellow men. Those psychologists who undertake the systematic assessment of individual differences among humans are primarily concerned with discovering the source of and the relationships among the many varieties of individual differences. Such psychologists, as scientists, look for ways of simplifying and ordering the complex phenomena of individual differences. As scientists, they search for unifying schema which will permit greater understanding of the magnitude, the sources, and the modifiability of specific characteristics as well as the interrelationships among them.

The nature-nurture problem. The obvious and marked range of human talents and other characteristics raises the challenging problem of the origins of these individual differences. In what respects are these differences a function of heredity and to what extent are they a function of variations in diet, climate, early childhood training, schooling, and a host of other experiences determined largely by the particular physical and cultural environment in which a person is born and lives? Without benefit of elaborate assessment procedures, one can see that certain human characteristics, such as skin color, are markedly determined by heredity. But when one considers another physical characteristic, height, the answer is not so obvious. It is apparent that tall parents tend to have tall children; but the relationship between the height of fathers and sons, for instance, is not a perfect one, and any precise estimate of the degree of this relationship requires (1) that height be accurately measured, (2) that large samples of parents and their children be studied, and (3) that appropriate statistical methods be used for analyzing the data obtained. Although tall fathers tend to have tall sons, the *average height* of the sons of tall fathers tends to be less than the average height of their fathers; and the average height of the sons of short fathers tends to be greater than the average height of their fathers. This tendency of children to be nearer the overall average than are their fathers was discovered by the British scientist Sir Francis Galton and designated by him, *filial regression.* After Galton had plotted the heights of fathers and their sons on a graph, he asked his statistician friend, Karl Pearson, to develop a generally applicable index of the degree of relationship between any two variables. The result was the coefficient of correlation (see Hays, 1967b), an extremely valuable tool to assessment psychologists. Because of its initial application to the study of *filial regression,* the symbol for this coefficient of correlation is "r."

Even though the height of children is positively correlated with (i.e., tends to be similar to) the heights of their parents, heredity does not nearly account for all of the individual differences in height. Some of the variability in height is the result of variations in diet, in eating habits, and in amounts and kinds of exercise—all of which are environmental variables. And, as might be expected, weight is more influenced by environmental variables than is height.

What about intellectual ability? Galton was also much concerned with this question (Galton, 1870); he collected data that led him to conclude that intelligence, like height, tends to run in families. Later, however, a number of investigators pointed out that more able parents typically provide their children with a more stimulating home environment and with more and better education than do parents of lesser ability. Some argued therefore that it is superior environment rather than superior heredity which results in the generally superior performance of the children of superior parents. Again, any scientifically sound estimate of the relative contributions of heredity and environment calls for the accurate measurement of the characteristic, and many of the early developments in the measurement of intellectual abilities were stimulated by scientists concerned with the nature-nurture issue. Interest in this problem has been revived recently by the widespread concern with the effect of poorer homes, communities, and schools on underprivileged groups in society (Dreger and Miller, 1960).

The degree to which a human characteristic is determined by genes or molded by environment is a fascinating issue regardless of the characteristic or trait in question, e.g., musical ability, honesty, morals, political attitudes, longevity. In almost any group, one will typically find equally strongly held convictions that nature or nurture is predominant in determining any particular human characteristic. Unfortunately, such arguments usually cannot be settled by reference to sound factual data, primarily because, as yet, no procedure has been developed for assessing the characteristic with the accuracy and fidelity necessary to permit definitive research on the question.

Students especially interested in the nature-nurture problem will find useful discussions of the methodology of such research and also summaries of the present state of knowledge in Fuller and Thompson (1960) and Vandenberg (1966).

Sex, race, and cultural differences.   One of the most obvious and hence easily accessible characteristics of human beings is biological sex. Except for the rare hermaphrodite, biological sex is readily assessed and is usually one of the earliest assessments made of each human being. When the obstetrician announces "It's a boy" or "It's a girl," this assessment initiates a series of differential ways in which the child will be treated: the name it will receive, the kind of toys it will be given, the games it will be encouraged to play, the kind of clothes it will wear. Later on, the child's sex will establish approved types of schooling and occupational choice, and behavior, especially in courtship.[1]

Research on the fascinating problem of sex differences is methodo-

[1]The "appropriate" roles of men and women are not necessarily the same in all cultures. For example see Mead (1949).

logically related to the nature-nurture problem: To what extent are the sex differences due to biological and physiological differences in men and women, and to what extent are they the result of the very different environmental and cultural influences impinging first on boys and girls and later on men and women in any given society?

The question of race differences poses another intriguing set of problems. Much of the writing on this subject has been by persons already convinced regarding either the superiority of one race or the equality of all races; all too little writing has been based on an objective evaluation of empirical data. The question of whether there are race differences is intimately related to the nature-nurture issue, since, typically, members of the dominant race in any society are more affluent and hence able to provide for their children a rich set of childhood and educational experiences that are not available to children of less privileged groups. Some authors, impressed by the lack of equality in educational and vocational opportunities for children of underprivileged groups, argue the extreme position that there are no biological racial differences with respect to any psychological characteristic. While such an egalitarian ideal may in fact be the case, we must admit, as of the present, that the essential facts regarding both sex and race differences are simply not known. Only when we have (1) assessments uninfluenced by nurture or (2) societies in which the sexes and the races have truly equal educational, vocational, economic, and social opportunities will it be possible to get factual answers regarding either sex or race differences.

Present knowledge permits us to say with confidence that the differences among persons of the same sex or race are very much greater than the differences between their average characteristics. For all characteristics there is a great deal of overlap in the distributions of measures of men and women or of persons of two different races; *in fact, the overlap is so great that if one knows only an individual's sex or race, one can tell little or nothing about him on any other characteristic.*

Age differences—the life cycle. Another field of investigation in which the assessment of human characteristics is critically important involves the study of changes associated with age. Attention was first given to the rapid development of abilities and other characteristics during the first few years of life, but, more recently, psychologists have also turned their attention to changes accompanying the aging process. As with research on sex and race differences, complex research designs are needed to separate the effects of simply growing up, or growing older, and the effects of environmental variables.[2]

---

[2]Anastasia (1958) and Tyler (1956) both provide extremely useful summaries of the fascinating field of individual and group differences.

The organization of personality. One of the most intriguing psycho-logical problems, from the standpoint of scientific understanding, is that of the patterns of relationships among the many human characteristics that are assessable. Already we have noted the interest in the relationship of genetic and environmental variables to human characteristics and in the possibility of differences associated with sex and race. But these reflect only a few of the thousands of possible relationships of interest. In fact, the moment one considers any two characteristics and notes the great individual differences with respect to them, two challenging ques-tions arise: (1) Are the two variables related, that is, is there a tendency for a person who ranks high on one of them, for example, intelligence, to be above (or below) average on the other, for example, musical ability? (2) If there is a relationship between any two variables, what is the most likely explanation for it? When one considers only two characteristics at a time, there is but one relationship involved. However, as the number of variables increases, the possible number of relationships goes up rapidly, the exact number of pairwise relationships being

$$\frac{n(n-1)}{2}$$

where "*n*" is the number of variables involved. For sample numbers of characteristics, the possible number of relationships are as follows:

NUMBER OF CHARACTERISTICS	NUMBER OF RELATIONSHIPS
2	2
3	3
4	6
5	10
10	45
20	190
50	1225
100	4950

From the above, it is obvious that the search for meaningful patterns of interrelationships among large numbers of characteristics presents an extremely challenging field of investigation.

PRACTICAL REASONS FOR ASSESSMENT

While scientists are seeking answers to the kinds of questions just discussed, every individual is confronted with the necessity of assessing the characteristics of those persons with whom he associates. Likewise, every organization finds it essential to recognize and deal with wide differences among its members, whether they be students, applicants, or employees. Let us now look briefly at some common everyday situations in which the need for assessment is based on very practical considerations.

The choice of friends and associates.   The informal but important processes of assessment begin in early childhood and may be observed in any nursery school. Each child typically forms strong friendships with a few selected members of his group, is generally neutral to others, and shows a definite dislike for still other children. He is not able to verbalize the basis for his likes and dislikes of other children, but obviously he perceives real differences among them. Only as he grows older does he learn the language necessary to name the characteristics that result in him liking one person and disliking another.

Throughout life, each of us is faced with the practical necessity of making similar discriminations among our fellow men before deciding what sort of personal relationship we wish to establish with each of them. The decision to become close friends is ordinarily made over an extended period of time and involves many opportunities for mutual assessment on the part of the two persons involved; furthermore, it is a decision that can be reversed, if, on the basis of further mutual assessment, one or both members of the pair become disenchanted with the relationship. Decisions with respect to other types of associates are sometimes less easily reversible, as with business associates and marital partners.

The choice of marital partners.   Perhaps the most critical assessment for most individuals is that involved in the choice of a marital partner. Marriage, the most intimate of human relationships, may bring happiness or misery to the man and woman involved; furthermore, the choice of a mate determines in part the kind of children the marriage will produce— whether one considers genetically determined traits or those primarily resulting from patterns of child rearing.

In American society, the initial assessment of prospective marriage partners ordinarily occurs first in the selection of dating partners from among a field of acquaintances. Later, the field is typically narrowed further by "steady dating" and if the boy and girl continue to find one another a suitable prospective mate, the relationship moves to a period of engagement and eventual marriage. The fact that many engagements are broken before marriage suggests that the assessment that occurred before the engagement was less than adequate. And while other conditions are also operative, the tragic fact that approximately one marriage out of four ends in divorce suggests that the total process of premarital assessment is often less than adequate as a basis for this important decision.

Educational and vocational counseling.   In spite of the democratic ideal of equal educational and vocational opportunities for all children, the extent of individual differences in learning ability among young children results in the necessity of providing different kinds of educational experiences from the first grade throughout the period of formal education. A few children learn to read even before they enter public school; others, not until they are seven or eight; and some never learn to read. Later, equally marked differences appear with respect to the ability to comprehend mathematics, science, literature, and philosophy and to compete in athletic, dramatic, musical, and other extracurricular activities.

Traditionally in the United States it was believed that the most appropriate educational practice was that of offering the same curriculum to all students and promoting to the next grade only those who had mastered the subject matter. The result was that some children remained two or even more years in the same grade and eventually dropped out of school. More recently, educational practice has shifted to keeping children of the same age in groups, which means annual promotions regardless of individual levels of educational achievement. Unless this practice is accompanied by highly differentiated curricula and teaching methods, it serves only to further emphasize original differences in the children's aptitudes for educational achievement. Therefore, larger school systems typically use what has been termed the multiple-track system, which recognizes frankly the marked differences among children with respect to their ability to master subject-matter content. This system involves the use of methods of assessment, placement, and promotion that permit each child to progress as fast and as far up the educational ladder as his abilities permit.

Since many vocations tend to have certain minimal educational entrance requirements, educational counseling and placement are inextricably linked with vocational counseling and planning. For example, it is hardly wise for a boy who cannot learn high school algebra to plan to become an engineer. Instead he might become a first-rate mechanic or technician. Similarly, a girl who has not learned the basic skills of English grammar and composition by the eighth grade should probably not seriously consider any vocation requiring a college degree. She might make an excellent practical nurse, but it is unlikely that she will be able to complete a collegiate nursing program.

Assessment procedures can be greatly helpful in assigning children to educational programs where they can experience success rather than failure and in counseling them with respect to realistic vocational goals. As we shall see, no method of assessment for educational and vocational counseling is perfect, and any method can be badly misused, i.e., used in a manner that is unfair to the child concerned. Wisely used, assessment methods can greatly reduce the frequency of failure and increase the probability of successful personal and vocational adjustment.

The selection, classification, and promotion of personnel. Just as human beings differ markedly from each other in myriad ways, so the roles differ which they play in life. We have already noted the markedly different roles expected of men and women in most societies. Equally important are the highly differential demands of the different occupations and professions with respect to human characteristics. Consider the contrasts between the abilities, skills, and temperament required of a janitor, sales manager, test pilot, judge, waitress, laboratory technician, editor of a fashion magazine, or teacher. The same abilities, skills, and personality characteristics required for success in any of these job roles might lead to failure, frustration, and unhappiness in another. For this reason, good assessment procedures are essential in the matching of persons and jobs.

Assessment procedures are also essential to any employer who wishes to increase the efficiency of his organization through better selection and classification of personnel. *Selection* occurs whenever there are more applicants for a job than there are positions available, since an employer is able to hire those who appear most likely to perform well on the job. An employer who knows the characteristics essential for good performance in each job and has the necessary techniques for assessing these essential characteristics is in a more favorable position to select productive employees than if he must select among applicants on a random basis. An industry that uses effective techniques of personnel selection is, therefore, likely to be more efficient than one which does not utilize such procedures.

Selection is possible only when there are more applicants than jobs. During periods when there is a shortage of manpower—periods of wartime production or other peaks of industrial effort—employers may be confronted with the necessity of hiring all the men they can get and then trying to assign each man to the type of work for which he is best qualified. The effort to maximize the fit between men and jobs within an organization is called *classification*. It requires both the specification of essential requirements for each type of work and the assessment of employees with respect to the characteristics needed on the several jobs. Classification, or re-classification, is also a necessary personnel practice in those situations where certain types of jobs are eliminated because of changes in manufacturing processes and the employer has a moral or contractual obligation to reassign displaced employees to new jobs within the organization.

The selection of persons for key roles in society. The selection of properly qualified persons increases in importance with the responsibility of the job to be performed. Long before the days of modern assessment techniques, most societies developed some type of practical assessment procedure for selecting their chiefs of state, their key government officials, their judges, etc. Traditionally, the position of chief of the government was typically filled by hereditary succession; more recently, in the democratic countries, both the chiefs of the government and other members of the legislative bodies have been elected by popular vote.

However, in modern complex societies, there are other key positions for which traditional methods of selection do not seem adequate. These are positions with such obviously critical responsibilities that psychologists and members of other professions are asked to use modern assessment tools in order to assure the selection of the best qualified persons to fill the key roles. One example already noted above was the OSS selection program for critical special assignment during World War II. Similarly, as larger aircraft were developed, much effort was spent on the selection of military pilots, thereby decreasing serious pilot error and the loss of men and equipment. Considerable attention was also paid to the selection of other military personnel with heavy responsibilities, such as submarine officers, and men who operated new and complex equipment like radar. The success of these programs for selecting military personnel during World War II encouraged the continued application of elaborate assessment techniques for the selection of personnel to carry out unusually demanding or hazardous missions. For example, the U.S. Navy makes a special effort to select suitable personnel for assignment to Antarctica, a mission in which the failure of a single individual would be most unfortunate, both for him and for the organization. Perhaps the most elaborate of the recent special assessment programs is that involved in the selection of astronauts. A less elaborate but nonetheless important program of assessment by a governmental agency is that of the Peace Corps. The selection of applicants and the assignment of each volunteer to a particular job and country is done in a manner that will result in the greatest probability of success in the unique and demanding role of a Peace Corps volunteer.

The diagnosis of human malfunction. The most familiar example of the practical need for assessment is medical diagnosis. When an individual is ill, he asks his physician to examine (i.e., to assess) him in an effort to determine the basis of his illness and thus to prescribe appropriate treatment. However, physical illness is only one of many situations in which human beings do not function as effectively as they should. Consider also the first-grade child who experiences difficulty in learning to read, the teen-age youngster whose school performance is considerably below his ability level, the college student who is unable to make educational or vocational decisions, the young man or woman who is unable to achieve a satisfactory social adjustment, the husband and wife whose marriage is going on the rocks, the individual who is unable to get along with his fellow workers on the job—all of these are examples of people performing in less than optimal fashion. While such persons are not "sick" in a physical or medical sense, they are all suffering from conditions that should be assessed and, if possible, alleviated.

Finally, there are people in every society who experience psychological breakdowns of short duration. And there are those who suffer from some form of mental disease that requires extended periods of hospitalization and treatment. Unfortunately, effective methods of treatment have not yet been developed for all of these afflictions of mankind, but the probability of effective treatment is greatly enhanced by a careful and accurate assessment of an individual's condition using the wide variety of psychological assessment techniques that have been developed to supplement those characteristically used by psychiatrists. When psychologists use their tools to evaluate the psychological functioning (and malfunctioning) of disturbed individuals, the assessment process is typically called psychodiagnosis.

IN CONCLUSION

Assessment is defined as the evaluation of human characteristics. Because human beings exhibit such an extensive range or variability with respect to almost every characteristic which one can name, many different groups of scientists (anthropologists, geneticists, psychologists, sociologists, etc.) have been intrigued by the sources of these extreme differences and have expended much effort in an attempt to determine (1) the degree to which the variability in each of many traits is a function of nature or nurture and (2) the relationship of such variability to sex, race, and age. Because of the very large number of traits which make up the human personality, still other scientists, psychologists especially, have been concerned with the organization of the personality as a whole—i.e., the relationships among characteristics. On the practical side, the fact that human beings differ so much one from another means that they are simply not interchangeable. Some will do one kind of work better than others; and even though two people hold the same type of position, they may still perform very differently. From the standpoint of the satisfaction of the individual as well as from that of the effective functioning of society as a whole, it is highly desirable that everyone find a role in society that will maximally use his abilities and personality characteristics but will not make demands on him that he cannot fulfill. Properly utilized assessment procedures hold much promise for contributing to this more perfect matching of persons and societal roles.

Psychologists and other professional persons concerned with evaluating human beings differ greatly in their assessment practices— with respect to the number and kinds of characteristics which they assess, in their methods of assessment, and in the language they use in describing the individuals they assess. Certain of these differences in practice grow out of differences in theoretical orientation; others result from differences in the professional training received; and still others are probably a function of personality characteristics of the assessors themselves. For example, professional persons with a strong psychoanalytical orientation are likely to rely heavily on a long series of interviews to get to know a person, to evaluate him with respect to characteristics regarded as important in psychoanalytic theory, and to report their assessment in the form of an interpretive essay. At the opposite extreme, some psychologists are convinced that the most useful accurate assessment of individuals comes from the administration of several machine-scored objective tests, the results of which may be reported simply as a profile of a person's scores on the variables measured. In this chapter we shall be concerned with what characteristics are potentially assessable. Subsequent chapters will deal with the different methods that are used to assess them.

As was noted in Chapter 1, all modern languages are rich in the number and variety of terms used to describe human beings and their behavior. This is appropriate because the human personality has so many facets, and the variability of persons is great with respect to each of them. The fact that no two persons are ever exact duplicates makes for a much more interesting world than would be the case if there were only two or three completely standardized varieties of persons, but it also makes for complications whenever we attempt to assess our fellow man. However, just as no two persons are exactly alike, neither are they completely different. We are all sufficiently alike to justify the classification *homo sapiens* and thus to be placed in a biological classification different from those of dogs, snakes, and mice!

TYPES

The great variation among persons has led on the one hand to the development in our language of an extremely long list of adjectives and on the other hand to many schemes for classifying or pigeonholing people into a small number of types.

Because of the great usefulness of the Linnean, or binomial, system for classifying all living things first by genera and then by species, it is not surprising that many similar schemes have been proposed for sorting and labeling humans: by the color of their skin, by their place of birth, by their language, by the level of their civilization, or by their physique.

The oldest known typology for the classification of persons by their psychological characteristics was employed by the Greek physician Hippocrates about 400 B.C. He believed that there were four kinds of body fluids called humours: blood, phlegm, yellow bile, and black bile and that each person's temperament was determined by the relative amounts of each of these four humours in his body. An excess of blood was thought to produce a *sanguine* temperament (hopeful, optimistic); an excess of phlegm was associated with a *phlegmatic* personality (calm, listless); too much black bile was thought to produce a *melancholic* individual; too much yellow bile was considered the basis for a *choleric* temperament (irritable, impatient).

More recently, there have been two major proposals for classifying persons into *constitutional types*. Both make physique the initial basis for typing and assert that certain psychological characteristics are associated with certain physical characteristics, since presumably both are hereditary. The first of these was proposed in 1925 by Kretschmer, a German psychiatrist. He argued that all persons can be classified into one of four types of body build:

1. pyknic—short, stocky, full chest, short hands and feet;
2. athletic—better proportioned, well developed bones and muscles, large hands and feet;
3. leptosome—tall, slender, narrow chest, long narrow hands and feet;
4. dysplastic—incompatible mixtures of the other three types.

Being a psychiatrist, Kretschmer was initially interested in the relationship between his physical types and kinds of mental diseases. He collected data to show that persons diagnosed as schizophrenic were preponderantly leptosomes whereas psychotics who were diagnosed as manic depressives were usually pyknics. On the basis of this evidence, he extended his theory to include nonpsychotic persons; he contended that the leptosomic body type is associated with a schizothymic personality (quiet, withdrawn, timid, and humorless) and the pyknic body build is associated with a cyclothymic personality (social, genial, outgoing, practical).

Unfortunately, Kretschmer's simple typology did not prove to be very useful, since only a small proportion of any group is readily assignable to one of the major body types. Even more damaging to his theory and system was the subsequent discovery that most of the association between body build and mental disease is due to marked age differences of the patients in the diagnostic categories studied by Kretschmer.

A more recent and considerably more flexible schema for constitutional typing was proposed by an American physician, Sheldon, in 1942. According to Sheldon, there are three dimensions of body build, each associated with corresponding temperaments:

PHYSIQUE	TEMPERAMENT
Endomorphy—soft roundness, overdevelopment of the digestive viscera.	Viscerotonic—relaxed, love of eating, sociable.
Mesomorphy—rectangular, muscular, strong.	Somatotonic —energetic, assertive, courageous.
Ectomorphy—longness, fragility, large brain and nervous system.	Cerebrotonic—restrained, introvertive.

Each of these three physical components is rated on a seven point scale, and a person's *somatotype* is reported as a three-digit index; for example, an extreme ectomorph would have a somatotype of 7-1-1. Thus, Sheldon's system allows for a very much larger number of body types than did Kretschmer's. Furthermore, if one rates the three components of temperament on a similar seven point scale, one can readily determine the degree of relationship between rated somatotype and rated temperament. Sheldon has reported extremely close associations, as predicted by his theory. However, his claims have not been supported by the findings of other independent researchers.

The use of types to categorize people is not necessarily associated with body build. Thus, the psychoanalytic theory proposes three types of personality: oral, anal, and genital. While these types and their names have their origin in the manner in which developing children are believed to handle the pleasurable experiences associated with eating, elimination, and sexual stimulation, they are regarded as characterizing a much wider range of behavior; e.g., an oral person is alleged to be dependent, and an anal person is supposed to be stingy. Jung, another psychoanalyst, who disagreed with Freud and developed his own variant of psychoanalytic theory, proposed an even simpler typology—that all persons be characterized as belonging to one of two types: introverts and extroverts.[1]

Relatively few ideas for categorizing people into types have been proposed by psychologists. The famous American William James suggested that people be categorized as the explosive vs. the obstructed-will

[1]See Blum (1953).

types with respect to voluntary actions and as the tender versus the tough-minded types in their approach to life.

Typing is the most typical mode of assessment employed by the ordinary person, who fancies that he thus simplifies his social world by classifying his associates into a few pigeonholes. Of course, the names associated with popular types are not any of those listed above. Examples of lay terms used to denote perceived types include bookworm, beatnik, hippie, teeniebopper, daredevil, dope, egghead, killjoy, sad sack, and jerk.

Essentially, any typological scheme for classifying humans must identify a few salient characteristics of the type and overlook many other aspects of the person. Such systems have considerable popular appeal, but they are neither adequate nor promising for the development of a science of personality or for use in practical problems requiring the assessment of human characteristics. Although it is usually possible to find a few pure examples of any proposed type, the fact is that most people simply do not fit clearly into any of the few categories proposed. For example, most people are neither introverts nor extroverts but possess characteristics of both types. Even Jung was eventually forced to recognize that there are several varieties of introverts and of extroverts.

Before leaving this discussion of types, we should note that there are a few human characteristics for which a system of typing is not only useful but quite proper, that is, a few characteristics which permit all persons to be sorted into one of a limited number of mutually exclusive categories. One example is blood typing—a person's blood is Type A, B, AB, or O. Another instance is typing according to the ability to taste phenyl-thio-carbamide (PTC), a crystal which to most people is quite bitter, but to others has no taste whatsoever (in other words, all people are either tasters or non-tasters of PTC). Both of these characteristics are known to be genetically determined, and both are relatively specific characteristics of persons. When we turn to the broader and generally more interesting characteristics in which people differ, we find far more variations than are provided for by any simple typological scheme.

TRAITS

Thus far, we have spoken of the assessment of human characteristics with the understanding that the word "characteristic" may refer to any aspect of the human organism and personality. Because simple typologies do not provide an adequate framework for describing human beings, we now introduce a more technical term: *trait*. Following Guilford, we shall define a trait as "any distinguishable, relatively enduring way in which one individual differs from another" (Guilford, 1959). So defined, trait is a very broad and useful concept. A trait may be as general as the tendency to participate or not participate actively in a wide variety of social situations or as narrow as the taste for particular kinds of food.

To be useful, however, certain minimum requirements must be met. A trait

1. must be a characteristic on which persons differ,
2. must be sufficiently identifiable so that different observers can agree reasonably well on how much (or little) of the characteristic an individual has or displays, and,
3. must show some degree of consistency over time, that is, the relative amount of characteristic must not change radically in a person from moment to moment or day to day.

The number of traits by which human beings might be assessed is very large, but there is far from complete agreement regarding either their number or the names that should be attached to them. It is useful, however, to note nine broad *modalities* (classes) of traits which are currently of interest to psychologists and to the users of assessment procedures.

The first two modalities are sometimes called somatic traits since they primarily reflect aspects of the form and functioning of the human being as a biological organism.

MORPHOLOGICAL TRAITS

Examples of morphological traits are height, weight, foot size and a number of more refined measures and indices developed by physical anthropologists. Some psychologists do not regard such traits as belonging to the domain of personality. Whether they do or not, these are characteristics with respect to which people differ greatly; and certain morphological traits, such as height and weight, are known to be related to other aspects of personality, especially that of self-concept.

PHYSIOLOGICAL TRAITS

Physiological traits are descriptive of the internal behavior of the individual—his heart rate, blood pressure, body temperature, basal metabolic rate, EEG, etc. Such measures vary widely from person to person. *Changes* in physiological measures also vary widely when people are subjected to physical or psychological stresses.

In contrast with these two classes of somatic traits, each of the remaining seven modalities involves traits which are involved in or reflect aspects of psychological behavior. The next two refer primarily to the abilities of individuals to behave and perform.

APTITUDES

An aptitude refers to a potential ability to perform. Conceptually, even before they have had an opportunity to acquire a particular type of skill or achievement, people differ widely in their aptitudes for different kinds of performance. Since the variety of possible performances is great, the possible list of aptitudes is long. It includes, among many others:

Scholastic aptitude—those abilities needed to succeed in school. Because of the nature of the traditional curriculum, scholastic aptitude is often further broken down into verbal and mathematical abilities.

Mechanical aptitude—the kind of ability that enables someone to acquire a superior understanding of mechanical principles and/or the use of tools.

Athletic aptitude—the combination of body build, perceptual ability, and muscular strength and coordination required to perform well in one or more sports.

Musical aptitude—the ability to learn to play an instrument or to compose music.

Other artistic aptitudes—the ability to create artistic products—to sing, to act—or to appreciate the aesthetic works of others.

Clerical aptitude—the ability to learn such skills as filing, typing, and shorthand.

SKILLS AND ACHIEVEMENTS

Just as people differ markedly with respect to their aptitudes, they also vary widely with respect to the maximum level of performance that they achieve. In general, one's aptitude sets a limit both on the rate of learning and on the maximal level of accomplishment, but there is far from a one-to-one relationship between aptitude and level of performance. Skills and knowledge are acquired only through practice and study, and one must be motivated to apply one's aptitudes to the acquisition of skills and knowledge. Resulting as they do from the combined effect of aptitude and practice, individual differences in levels of performance and achievement are likely to be even greater than differences in aptitude.

Such differences are also enhanced because one does not have the time and energy to learn everything, even if one has the necessary aptitudes. Thus, of two students with equal aptitude for learning a foreign language, one may choose to study French and the other German; or of two students with equal musical aptitude, one may choose the piano and the other the violin.

The most systematic assessment of achievement occurs in the field of education, in which standardized tests have been developed for measuring a wide array of skills and knowledge. Such tests, called educational achievement tests, are available for all age levels from the first grade to graduate school. Perhaps the most familiar examples to college undergraduates are the college board tests, which permit the assessment of achievement in several subject-matter fields. These assessments are independent of the high school that a student attended and independent of the grading practices of his school.

A performance trait showing extremely wide variations in perform-ance is reading skill. Among college freshmen, even those in highly selective colleges, differences both in reading rate and in reading comprehension are enormous. Because reading constitutes an essential skill for further education, many colleges and universities have estab-lished programs for assessing reading skills and assisting deficient students in improving their reading skills.

Standard assessment procedures are also available for typing and stenographic proficiency and for skill in transmitting and receiving radio code.

For most of the hundreds of human skills and achievements, no standardized assessment procedures have been developed. Although extremely wide ranges of performance are recognized, they are more typically assessed "on the job." In the case of athletic skills, one's compe-tence is assessed by the ability "to make the team," to score points, and so forth. In the case of artistic performances, there are tryouts, critical reviews, and prizes. With respect to certain skills, society is content to demand a demonstration of only a minimal level of performance, as, for example, in automobile driver tests.

Performance traits include not only relatively specific skills such as the ability to drive, to read, to operate a lathe, to speak a foreign language, but also broader social skills, such as the ability to converse easily, to dance, and to discuss current events in detail. Whether per-formance traits are systematically assessed or not, it is important to remember that people differ greatly with respect to all of them and that these are very important aspects of the functioning of individuals in society.

Although it is relatively easy to conceptualize the difference between an aptitude and performance, they are often difficult to assess with complete independence. In fact, measures of achievement, made after an initial period of training, often provide the best assessment of aptitude for later achievement in the same field.

The next four modalities are sometimes called *motivational* traits; all reflect the ways in which persons choose to utilize their aptitudes, time, and energies.

DRIVES

Drives are deep-seated continuing tendencies to attain certain conditions or rewards. They include not only the universal biological drives, induced by the need for food, water, sex, and activity, but also the more purely psychological ones, induced by needs for attention, excitement, achievement, respect, and dominance. Such needs may be either conscious or unconscious.

INTERESTS

Interests refer to the preferences of a person among the wide array of things, persons, and activities in his environment. In general, the interests of an individual are reflected both in his expressed likes or dislikes and, when a choice is available, in the ways that he chooses to use his time and energy. Thus, two persons with the same aptitude for mechanical activities may vary greatly in their interest in mechanical things and hence in the level of the mechanical skills that they develop.

VALUES

Values refer to broad classes of objects, experiences, and/or goals toward which different persons strive with widely varying degrees of effort and dedication. Thus painters are characterized by high aesthetic values, businessmen by strong economic or utilitarian values, ministers and social workers by religious or socio-humanitarian values.

ATTITUDES

Attitudes refer to the opinions and beliefs that a person holds regarding objects, people, activities, and social policies and practices. They are reflected in the pro, con, or neutral stances *vis-à-vis* such widely varied things as the church, civil rights, states' rights, the income tax, birth control, and members of other races.

TRAITS OF TEMPERAMENT

This is perhaps the most general and the least well defined of the nine trait modalities; more positively, temperament refers to dispositional traits such as a person's tendency to be cheerful or pessimistic, even-tempered or moody, self-confident or insecure, outgoing or withdrawn, impulsive or controlled in his behavior. Obviously, such traits are extremely important both for the adjustment of the individual and for his interactions with others.

This completes our brief and admittedly incomplete survey of the trait modalities in which people differ from one another. There is a far from uniform agreement as to how many different traits there are in each of the several modalities, but certainly anything approaching a well-rounded or complete assessment of a person would require the determination of his position on a representative sample of traits from each of the nine modalities. The human being is a very complex organism, both biologically and psychologically, and this is the chief reason why no simple set of types is adequate to describe a person fully.

PSYCHODIAGNOSTIC CATEGORIES

While psychologists concerned with assessment are overwhelmingly committed to the use of the trait approach (as contrasted with typing or pigeonholing), there is one field of assessment practice in which the trait approach is not yet fully accepted. This is psychodiagnosis, a specialty in which a clinical psychologist, usually functioning in a medical-psychiatric setting, is concerned with assessing the basis of human malfunctioning. Because of the dramatic successes of medical researchers in the identification of disease entities, the causes of disease, and effective therapeutic procedures, psychiatrists confronted with problems of behavioral malfunction are oriented to categorizing—i.e., diagnosing—the patient as suffering from a specific disease entity, such as neurosis, schizophrenia, paranoia, etc. As with other typologies, it is always possible to find relatively pure examples, but rapidly mounting evidence makes it increasingly doubtful that most of the pathologies in the domain of behavioral malfunction do in fact correspond to specific disease entities. More and more, therefore, psychologists working in medical settings are beginning to utilize the trait approach to provide fuller assessments of neuropsychiatric patients.

SOME IMPORTANT PROPERTIES OF TRAITS

Before considering (in the next chapter) the methods by which a person's traits are assessed, let us note several important aspects of the trait concept.

A trait is a continuum. A trait may be thought of as a dimension, i.e., a line made up of an infinite number of possible points, any one of which may be descriptive of some person with respect to the trait. Such a dimension has both an upper and lower limit within which all persons fall. As contrasted with a type, to which a person either belongs or does not belong, a trait continuum has some point that best describes every person.

Most traits are scalable. This statement implies that it is possible to derive scale units representing distances on the trait continuum. Whether the resulting scale corresponds to an ordinal, interval, or ratio scale (see Hays, 1967b) depends upon the operations involved in its assessment, the assumptions underlying these operations, and the nature of the statistical procedures used in defining the units of the scale.

Traits may be either unipolar or bipolar. Conceptually, a unipolar trait is one that extends from the lowest possible amount in any person to the greatest possible amount in any person. Graphically, such a trait would be represented as follows:

Trait X: ———————————————————————————
Low   High

Unipolar traits are most likely to be found among morphological and physiological variables, but the concept is equally applicable to aptitudes, performances, and some of the motivational traits for which some individuals possess very little aptitude or skill of a particular kind. For these trait modalities, however, it is difficult to conceptualize a person with absolutely none of the trait, that is, a "0" amount.

Among the traits of temperament, bipolar traits are far more typical. A bipolar trait is one in which the trait scale extends from one extreme of behavior through a neutral point and on to the extreme opposite. Here is an example of a bipolar trait:

Trait Y: ———————————————————————————
– Y   Neutral   + Y

The degree to which bipolar conceptions pervade our thinking is reflected in the fact that for almost every adjective in our language descriptive of a person there is an antonym, e.g., cheerful-pessimistic, dominant-submissive, friendly-unfriendly. On such scales the neutral position falls at a point descriptive of an individual whose behavior is such that he can be best characterized by a point midway between the two ends of the bipolar scale.

For most traits, there is general consensus regarding the "good" or "positive" end of the scale. For unipolar aptitude and performance traits, it is generally agreed that the more one has, the better. It is of interest that bipolar traits tend to have similar value loadings, that is, it is "better" to be friendly rather than unfriendly, cheerful rather than depressed, and cooperative rather than uncooperative. Note, however, that this is not true for all traits. For example, it is "better" to be of near average height than extremely tall or short, and most people prefer their friends to be neither too dominant nor too submissive!

Most trait continua are conceptualized as corresponding to interval scales of measurement. Numbers are often used to designate points on a trait continuum, but the resulting scale of measurement rarely meets the two requirements of a ratio scale: (1) an absolute zero corresponding to a complete absence of the trait, and (2) equal intervals. Except for certain morphological and physiological traits which are assessed by physical measures like length, weight, or cycles-per-second, the concept of an absolute zero point is not very meaningful; for example, it is difficult to conceive of a living person with absolutely no intelligence, initiative, or anxiety! In most instances, therefore, the zero point on any trait scale is a purely arbitrary one, just like "0 degrees" on a Fahrenheit or Centigrade thermometer. For unipolar traits, zero is often assigned to the lowest point on the continuum; for bipolar traits, zero is frequently assigned to the midpoint or neutral position on the scale, in which case other points are assigned plus or minus values, depending usually on the value judgments associated with the ends of the scale. The number of units into which trait scales are divided is also a purely arbitrary matter: It may be 3, 5, 7, 10, or some larger number. In general, however, an effort is made to divide the continuum into intervals of equal size. The result is that most traits are assessed on what are assumed to be interval scales, in order to permit the resulting measures to be used in statistical analyses. This means that while one may properly infer that the distance from 2 to 4 is the same as that from 4 to 6, one cannot assume that a value of 6 represents twice the amount of a trait represented by the value of 3—any more than one can conclude that a 60° (Fahrenheit) day is twice as warm as a 30°F day!

OBJECTIONS TO THE USE OF TRAITS AS A BASIS FOR ASSESSMENTS

Many persons, especially some psychologists and psychiatrists with a strong literary or psychoanayltic orientation, have been reluctant to accept the trait approach to personality assessment on the grounds that human beings are much too complex to be studied in terms of isolated trait dimensions. They argue that no matter how many traits are assessed, the resulting picture loses the essence of the individual under study. Such psychologists and psychiatrists tend to prefer the case-study, or global, approach to assessment and to report their findings in the form of a descriptive essay. Unfortunately, while such case studies often make fascinating reading, they are of relatively little use in research on personality because the form of the data does not permit the comparison of two persons or two groups of persons. Furthermore, this more literary unstructured approach has not yet been demonstrated to have any unique value in a wide variety of applied assessment situations (Sawyer, 1966).

Lest the reader be concerned that the trait approach to assessment loses the uniqueness of the individual, consider the following: Assume that we could assess persons only on 10 unrelated traits and that our techniques are so crude as to permit allocation of each person to but one of 10 points on each trait scale. How many unique profiles would be possible? The answer is 10^{10}, or ten billion! Since the possible number of traits we can assess is many times ten, and since many of them can be assessed on a scale with more than 10 scale units, there is the obvious possibility of finding a unique profile for every person; in fact, there would be literally millions of possible profiles with no person to correspond to them!

The problem, then, is not one of too few traits or potential profiles but of assessment procedures resulting in more data than the human mind can comprehend. Given billions of possible trait profiles, we need a schema for grouping similar ones into a much smaller number of useful categories.

WHAT TRAITS SHALL BE ASSESSED?

The answer to the question "What traits shall be assessed?" is simple: "It all depends on the purpose of the assessment, that is, on the nature of the research undertaken or on the kind of practical decision that must be made regarding the people who are assessed, whether in schools, in hospitals, in industry, in a military organization, etc." The Canadian humorist Stephen Leacock once wrote of the horseman "who got on his horse and rode away in all directions." It is equally ridiculous to attempt to assess "an individual as a whole," and it is extremely time consuming and expensive to undertake to assess someone equally well on all possible traits. In any given assessment situation, whether one is concerned with pure research or with an applied problem of selection and classification of personnel, the assessment psychologist must identify those traits most relevant to the problem and then utilize those techniques which have been demonstrated to provide the most accurate assessment of these traits. Thus, for example, an investigator concerned with sex differences in psychological needs would not be likely to assess his subjects on morphological traits. And, while morphological and physiological traits are probably relevant in the selection of astronauts, they are not likely to be appropriate to the selection of clerical personnel or college students.

ASSESSMENTS MUST BE INFERRED FROM BEHAVIOR

Certain morphological and physiological traits may be assessed by applying a physical measuring instrument directly to the dimension in which we are interested (e.g., using a tape measure to measure head girth or scales to measure weight). Most human traits, however, must be estimated or inferred indirectly from behavior. No matter how strongly we may be convinced of the reality of a given trait, such as "intelligence" or "initiative," it cannot be seen, felt, or otherwise sensed directly. Therefore, in the assessment of most traits, psychologists must rely completely on inferences based on the behavior of the individual. Methodologically, psychologists are in the same position as the physicist who wishes to measure temperature. Within a very limited range, temperature may be sensed directly by a human judge; however, such judgments are relatively inaccurate, and if an object is too cold or too hot, the human sense organs will be destroyed. Fortunately, there is a one-to-one relationship between temperatures and the behavior (expansion-contraction) of certain materials, hence temperatures can be accurately but *indirectly* measured over limited ranges by measuring the volume occupied by a given amount of mercury or alcohol. Extremely high or low temperatures, below the freezing point or above the boiling point of these liquids, can be similarly inferred from the expansion of metals.

Such simple one-to-one relationships between a dimension and behavior are relatively rare even in the physical sciences. When we consider the behavior of gases, three variables—temperature, volume, and pressure—covary as described by Boyle's Law. In even the simplest living organisms, behavior appears to be affected by many rather than one or just a few variables. At the human level, the situation is far more complex. It is doubtful that any specific behavior is a function of a single trait; instead, a behavioral response is likely to be influenced by two or more traits *and* by a wide variety of conditions in the person's immediate environment. Consequently, inferences regarding a person's position on any trait continuum must be made with great caution and with due consideration for a series of methodological issues, to be discussed later in this volume.

THE LOGIC OF MAKING TRAIT INFFRENCES FROM BEHAVIOR

All behavior is presumably a function of both the person and the situation to which he is responding. Assuming a known standardized situation, it is reasonable for us to infer that differences in behavior reflect differences in the trait structures of the individuals being observed. Assessment, then, involves the observation of the behavior of persons in defined situations and the inference of the position of each person on one or more trait continua.

In terms of our language structure, we describe behavior with verbs: Individual A *withdraws* his finger when pricked with a pin, *solves* a problem, *laughs* when confronted with certain pictures, *converses* with friends at a party, *offers* to help start a car belonging to a stranger. To further describe such behavior, we use adverbs or adverbial phrases, e.g., "A" withdraws his finger *quickly*; he solves the problem *brilliantly*, he laughs *heartily*; he converses *with enthusiasm*; he *spontaneously* offers to help start the car. Note that such adverbial modifiers apply only to the specific behavior in question; up to this point there have been no inferences about A as a person.

The next step, however, is a crucial one: Because A solved the problem brilliantly, we conclude that A is *brilliant* or *intelligent*; because he conversed with enthusiasm, we conclude that he is *sociable*; because he voluntarily offered to help start the car, he is *cooperative*. The moment we make this step—that is, shift from the use of verbs and adverbs for the description of specific behaviors to the use of adjectives to describe the behaving person—we have begun the process of assessing the individual.

The final step in the logical process involves the substitution of nouns for adjectives. For example, we not only judge A to be intelligent but also conclude that he has considerable *intelligence;* and because he is sociable, we judge him to rank high on the trait of *sociability*. Note that the trait of "intelligence" or "sociability" or any other trait expressed as a noun is a purely inferential construct. No one has ever seen, heard, or felt a trait; all traits are dimensions inferred from behavior.

WHAT KINDS OF BEHAVIOR SHALL BE USED FOR ASSESSMENT?

In view of (1) the potentially large number of personality traits that may be assessed, (2) the existence of very different theories of personality, (3) the absence of any consensus with respect to the naming of traits, and (4) the different purposes for which psychologists engage in personality assessment, we should not be surprised that there are wide differences both in opinion and in practice regarding the best and most useful methods of assessment. Psychologists are in agreement that assessment must be based on overt behavior, but there are extremely wide differences with respect to (1) the kinds of behavior used as a basis for such inferences, (2) the methods to be used in collecting behavioral data, and (3) the basis for making inferences from behavior to traits.

A useful classification of the kinds of data which may be used in assessment was proposed by Cattell (Cattell, 1957).

LIFE RECORD (L DATA)

This category potentially includes all of the behavior of an individual from birth to the time of assessment. But because there is no systematic record of most of the behavior of most people, life-record data are usually restricted to those aspects of a person's previous behavior for which there are objective records—baby book, school grades, and work history.

QUESTIONNAIRE (Q DATA)

As contrasted with other biological organisms, humans are capable of remembering many of their life experiences and reporting them in oral or written form. Direct questioning of a person thus elicits behavior which may be used as an alternative to recorded life behavior. However, because of the known individual differences in the ability to remember and to report accurately, and because of the possibility of motivated distortion in such reports (e.g., giving a socially desirable answer even though it is not the true one), Cattell proposes a further breakdown in questionnaire data:

Q_1—for which it is assumed that the individual is responding accurately and honestly and hence his answers to questions represent the "facts."
or,
Q_2—for which the answers a person gives to questions are not assumed to be true or false but simply treated as behavioral responses elicited in a particular situation and later evaluated as responses just as are responses to test items.

TEST (T DATA)

This category includes a wide variety of behavior elicited in an equally wide variety of test situations. All psychological test situations have certain common characteristics: (1) They are specifically designed to provide a more or less standard and known situation and to elicit certain kinds of responses; and (2) these responses are, in turn, used to make inferences about a trait or traits of the person tested. But, apart from these common basic characteristics, tests may and do vary greatly.

1. Tests vary with respect to their content, i.e., the kinds of responses they are designed to elicit and the traits to be evaluated. Certain tests are designed to assess intelligence; others, achievement; and still others, creativity, rigidity, anxiety, etc.

2. Some tests are designed to measure maximal performance (power); others, maximal rate (speed); still others, typical behavior of the individual when not instructed or motivated to perform maximally.

3. Tests vary in form. Some tests consist of oral questions and oral answers; others, oral questions and written answers; others, written questions and written answers. Some are administered individually; others, in groups. Some tests call for verbal responses; others, for other kinds of responses (drawing, performing a skill).

4. Tests vary in the degree of structure. This refers to the relative clarity or ambiguity of the total testing situation presented to the subject. A highly structured test is one in which subjects are presented with a well-defined task or set of tasks, as in reasoning problems, *and* are given equally specific instructions as to whether they should work as rapidly as possible, as accurately as possible, or should try to achieve some specified balance between speed and accuracy. Most aptitude and achievement tests are of this kind. At the other end of this continuum of "structuredness," the subject is presented with an extremely general situation and an almost equally general set of instructions. For example, in the well-known Rorschach Inkblot Test, the subject is merely shown an inkblot and asked, "What do you see?" or "What does it look like?" On the Thematic-Apperception Test (TAT), the subject is shown a picture and simply asked "to tell a story about the picture." Such relatively unstructured test situations are typical of the so-called "projective" tests. An almost equal lack of structure characterizes a course assignment such as "A theme will be due on Friday" or a selection interview which begins with: "Tell me something about yourself" (Coombs, 1953).

5. Tests vary in regard to objectivity. The objectivity-subjectivity dimension is closely associated with the structured-unstructured dimension just discussed, in that objective tests tend to be highly structured, and subjective tests, relatively unstructured. The objective-subjective continuum, however, emphasizes additional differentiating characteristics of tests. The first characteristic is the limited range of test responses permitted the subject. For example, when taking a true-false test, the subject has only one of three alternative responses: to mark an item "true," to mark it "false," or to omit it. By contrast, a subject asked to tell what he sees in an inkblot has an almost unlimited range of responses available to him, with respect to both the content of his response and the number of different responses which he makes. (He also, of course,

has the alternatives of making no response, or saying that the inkblot looks like nothing but an inkblot!) The second aspect of the objective-subjective continuum is concerned with the extent to which human judgment is involved in scoring or interpreting test responses. A highly objective test is much more likely to elicit comparable responses which can be scored the same regardless of who administers the test or scores the responses. By contrast, the subjects' responses on a highly subjective test may vary considerably, depending on who administers the test and decides the resulting score.

ALTERNATE STRATEGIES OF INFERRING PSYCHOLOGICAL MEANING FROM BEHAVIOR

Although there is almost complete agreement with the principle that human characteristics (with the previously noted exception of certain somatic and physiological traits) must be inferred from behavior, there are wide differences regarding the best method of making this crucial but necessary logical step. The remainder of this chapter describes various strategies currently employed by assessment psychologists in making such inferences.

THE RATIONAL STRATEGIES

Commonsense or nontheoretical (R_1). This strategy assumes that intelligent human 'beings, as the result of their shared cultural backgrounds, their common language, and their experiences in dealing with other persons, can infer psychological meaning from the behavior of persons they observe, whether in natural settings or in test situations. The simplest example of this occurs when we ask a friend, an associate, or a supervisor to evaluate a person on traits such as courtesy, honesty, promptness, or sociability. It is assumed that each rater uses these psychological dimensions with the same meaning. Further assumptions are (1) that each judge has had the opportunity to observe the subject in a variety of life situations, (2) that there is general agreement as to how each piece of observed behavior should be weighted, and (3) that the human mind is a reasonably accurate computer for arriving at a weighted average somewhat near the subject's true position on the trait being assessed. Similar assumptions are also involved whenever we ask a person to judge himself on one or more traits.

Another example of the commonsense strategy is the approach used by teachers in preparing a test or examination for their course. A teacher of American history is likely to feel that he knows not only the kinds of knowledge that should be sampled to assess achievement in his course but also, *a priori*, the "correct" answer to each question, how much each question should be weighted on a test, and how much each test or term paper should be weighted in arriving at a student's grade in the course. As every student knows, teachers vary widely with respect to the emphasis they place on facts versus principles and with respect to the weights they assign to quizzes, tests, term papers, and final examinations. Therefore, standardized educational tests are typically constructed not by a single individual but by a panel of experts who reach consensus regarding the content of the test (e.g., does this item assess achievement in American history or political science?), the form of the questions (true-false, multiple choice, completion, or essay), the "correct" responses, and the weights to be assigned to various parts of the test.

Still another example of reliance on the rational nontheoretical strategy is found in the construction of certain personality inventories—both in writing the questions and in deciding weights to be assigned to the responses. Thus, to the question "Do you often feel jittery?", which would seem, *a priori,* to tap the trait of anxiety, a "yes" answer would be rationally scored "plus" on a scale designed to measure the trait of anxiety. But the same response of "yes" to the item "I am rarely upset" would be scored minus. Available evidence indicates that intelligent persons with but little or no professional training show considerable agreement with respect both to the designation of inventory items which they believe to tap common traits and the appropriate sign of the "yes" or "no" response to each item.

Rational theoretical (R_2). This strategy of devising questionnaires or test items and deciding on the proper method of scoring them involves essentially the same operations as the commonsense strategy above, but with one very important difference: All decisions are presumably made within the framework of some theory of personality. In brief, the theory prescribes what traits or variables are to be assessed, what behaviors are the best indicators of these variables, and what weights (scores or interpretations) should be given to the responses elicited. Examples of personality tests based on this strategy include the Allport-Vernon-Linsey *Scale of Values* (1936), developed on the basis of Spranger's theory of values; the Edwards Personal Preference Schedule (1954), based on Murray's theory of needs; and Blum's Blacky Pictures (1950), based on psychoanalytic theory.

In general, the less unstructured an assessment technique is, the more it is likely to be based on one or the other of these rational strategies. Perhaps the most extreme example of the use of the rational strategy is the selection interview so widely used by educational institutions, industry, and government. In the typical selection interview, the interviewer tends to decide either before or during the interview (on the basis of his experience and/or his theoretical orientation) what questions he will ask each applicant and how he will weight an applicant's responses in assessing the characteristics he believes to be relevant to the position for which the applicant is being considered. While an interview may be highly structured, as when the same questions are asked of each candidate, many interviewers are convinced that they can learn more by "tailoring" each interview to the individual candidate.

Likewise, proponents of projective techniques tend to rely heavily on rational strategies. As has already been noted, projective techniques tend to be highly unstructured, that is, they present the subject with an ambiguous task which permits many alternative responses. The scoring—or more accurately, the coding—of a subject's responses may follow a carefully worked-out set of categories; and judges may be trained to agree reasonably well in classifying or coding subjects' responses. But interpretation, i.e., the process of inferring psychological-trait positions from responses, is likely to rely heavily on theories regarding the "meaning" of each category of responses.

THE EMPIRICAL STRATEGY

As contrasted with the rational strategies just discussed, the empirical strategy starts with the assumption that neither our commonsense nor our personality theories are adequate to enable us to decide, on an *a priori* basis, (1) which behaviors are related to the psychological variable that we wish to assess or (2) the proper scoring or weighting of the responses elicited in a test situation. Instead, those committed to the empirical strategy start with behavior in a real-life situation, in which groups of individuals show marked behavioral differences; then they search systematically for test behaviors which systematically discriminate between persons who behave or perform in grossly different ways. One of the best known assessment devices developed on the basis of the empirical strategy is the Minnesota Multiphasic Inventory (MMPI). The authors of this scale, a psychologist and a psychiatrist (Hathaway and McKinley), were concerned with assessing the degree to which a patient resembles normal persons and the degree to which he resembles persons with a variety of psychiatric diagnoses, both neurotic and psychotic. Many kinds of behavioral responses might discriminate between and among such persons, but the authors decided for practical reasons to use questions about the subject which he could answer "true" or "false." In compiling the list of more than 500 questions which were eventually included in the inventory, the authors relied heavily on their experience with normal persons and with many kinds of neuro-psychiatric patients; the authors also were probably influenced by the theories of psychopathology with which they were familiar. The critical difference between this empirical strategy and the rational strategies lies in the fact that with the empirical strategy a subject's responses to questions are regarded not as "facts" but merely as test responses. In the case of the MMPI, the decision to score a response as normal, paranoid, schizophrenic, etc., was based entirely on a comparison of the typical or modal response of different criterion groups. Both the relevance of items to given traits and the direction (sign) of the scoring were decided solely on the basis of the relative frequency of the response given by normal persons and the several categories of psychiatric patients. The empirical strategy demands that responses to each item be scored, not as common sense would dictate, nor as theory would predict, but rather in accordance with empirical evidence of truly discriminative test behaviors of the criterion groups. Regardless of the apparent relevance of an item, or the theoretically "schizophrenic response" to an item, it was scored for the trait of schizophrenia only if diagnosed schizophrenics tended to respond to it differently than did normal individuals.

Another well-known example of an assessment technique developed on the basis of the empirical strategy is the Strong Vocational Interest Blank (Strong, 1953). In developing this instrument, Strong assumed that men who selected different occupations and professions for their life work did so not only on the basis of differing aptitudes but also because they had different patterns of interests. First he assembled a self-report form of some 400 items. Subjects were asked to indicate whether they like, dislike, or are indifferent toward a large number of objects—school subjects, sports activities, kinds of people, kinds of activities, etc. Other items involve the subject's preferences for one or another of paired persons, things, or activities. Next, Strong identified large samples (200-300) of successful persons in many different professions and asked them to respond to these items. Items were scored for a given profession only if persons in that profession typically responded to the item differently than "men in general," i.e., all of his thousands of subjects. The result is that the score of an individual on any Strong scale reflects the degree to which a person's interests are typical of the unique pattern of behavioral responses of persons already successful in the profession. Some 50 different scales were thus empirically derived; hence, the SVIB yields a profile of these scores for each person.

Still other assessment devices constructed on the basis of the empirical strategy are the biographical inventories designed to predict performances in a situation. One of the earliest of these (unpublished) was an empirically scored application blank used in the selection of insurance salesmen. The essential aspects of this method will be clear from a brief description of a biographical inventory (BI) developed by the author to assess aptitude for flying. On the basis of his personal experience as a pilot and his conversations with many flight instructors, the author assembled a list of several hundred questions dealing with various experiences at home, in school, on the playground, on the job, etc. This questionnaire was administered to several hundred young men before they began a federally sponsored Civilian Pilot Training Program in 1940–42, and their responses were stored until after they had completed their training—or failed to do so. Then, for each question, a comparison was made of the typical response of the successful and unsuccessful trainees. Responses which were more characteristic of successful trainees were scored plus, and those more typical of unsuccessful trainees were scored minus. Scores on this inventory proved to be one of the most useful predictors of performance in flight training, first in civilian programs, and later in the U.S. Navy. A similar device was later developed and used by the U.S. Air Force.

THE FACTOR-ANALYTIC STRATEGY

The factor-analytic strategy of making the inferential leap from behavioral responses to hypothetical psychological traits or constructs takes its designation from its use and reliance on a complex set of statistical procedures known as factor analysis. Fortunately, it is not necessary that the reader comprehend the intricacies of factor-analytic techniques (or computational techniques) in order to understand the essence of this strategy. It is this: Behavioral responses should be grouped together, and inferences about traits should be made from responses only to the degree that behaviors covary, i.e., go with each other. The initial statistical procedure used is that of computing correlations between and among a large number of test behaviors and noting the magnitude (and the sign) of all correlations (see Hays, 1967b). Only to the degree that these behaviors (questionnaire responses, test scores, BI responses, etc.) tend to be highly correlated according to factor-analytic strategy, should one make similar inferences from different behavioral responses. Even though a personality theory says that trait X is equally likely to reflect itself in Behaviors A, B, C, D, and E, the factor-analytic strategy would combine these responses (e.g., add the scores) only if they tend to cluster in a factor analysis.

Factor-analytic strategy establishes not only a criterion for determining which responses shall be grouped in making inferences regarding a person's position on a trait but also a criterion for determining how many different traits may be inferred from any set of assessment data. It is permissible for one to conclude that a unique trait is being assessed by a subset of responses only to the extent that the responses are in fact (1) related to each other and (2) essentially unrelated to other subsets of responses.

The factor-analytic strategy does not by itself permit the identification or naming of the personality trait (or psychological construct) presumably responsible for the correlations among any subset of responses. This step, the naming and interpretation of the variable being measured, requires that the developer of the assessment instrument infer the nature of the trait that results in the covariation of any set of responses. Initially, this is done by a careful analysis of the correlated set of test items and the behaviors constituting the factor. In the long run, however, the proper label or meaning of any factor must be determined by the nature of its relationship with a wide variety of other behaviors: those elicited by other tests and those which occur in life situations (see Chapter 4, Construct Validity). Occasionally, a psychologist may be confronted with a set of correlated behaviors which obviously have a common "cause" but for which no obvious "explanation" is readily available. While he may be sure that the factor is real, he is probably wise to designate it by a letter or number until further research reveals more about the nature of the variable or trait.

Summarizing this brief review of the alternate strategies of inferring traits from behavior, let us note the advantages and disadvantages of each. The rational strategies are those which make the best sense to the layman and to many psychologists. One begins by assuming that one knows, *a priori*, what trait he wants to assess and what kinds of behavior of a person are indicative of this trait. *To the extent that these assumptions are justified,* one may construct a reasonably good assessment device using a rational strategy. However, these widely used strategies are accompanied by serious hazards:

1. The "trait" which one sets out to assess may not in fact be a single dimension but a combination of two or more independent components; yet nothing in the strategy or the operations will ever reveal this serious erroneous assumption.

2. Two psychologists may independently develop measures of the same assumed trait but end up with assessment instruments which, though yielding scores bearing the same label, are totally uncorrelated with each other. As an example, not only of the possibility but of the probability of such an unfortunate occurrence, consider the following: D. Applezweig, in a doctoral dissertation carried out under the author's direction, assessed "rigidity" in a group of subjects. She used six different measures of rigidity, each of which had been developed by a different psychologist using an *a priori* rational approach. Not one of these six measures was significantly related to any of the others (Applezweig, 1954). Unfortunately, a similar situation exists with respect to alternative available measures of other important psychological constructs.

3. Two psychologists who set out to measure different traits using

only rational strategies, may develop two presumably independent measures of two different variables which later research will show to be essentially the same. That this is more than a remote possibility is reflected in the fact that scores based on an early inventory that was designed to measure "neuroticism" correlated almost perfectly with scores from another early inventory designed to assess "introversion."

A psychologist relying on the empirical strategy, on the other hand, starts out by admitting that he is not sure what trait or traits he wishes to assess. His interest is in identifying behaviors (from L data, Q data, or T data) which enable him to discriminate between groups of persons who are obviously different: normal versus psychotic people, good vs. poor salesmen, or successful vs. unsuccessful candidates in a pilot training program. He may succeed in developing a useful assessment device for his purpose; but even though it "works," this strategy may yield no new basic knowledge regarding the personality traits being measured. Furthermore, one can never assume that an inventory that has been empirically keyed for one purpose is at all useful for an apparently similar assessment task. For example, a biographical inventory that measures "aptitude for selling life insurance" may or may not be useful in selecting automobile salesmen.

Many assessment psychologists who prefer the factor-analytic strategy begin by admitting they are not sure what trait or traits they are going to measure. Their goal is, first, to discover how many different traits may properly be inferred from any set of test behaviors and, second, to identify the appropriate subset of behaviors for making inferences about each trait. They may be confronted with traits that are not immediately identifiable, but they can be reasonably certain that each trait is a homogeneous dimension, i.e., independent of the others found.

It is obvious, from the above, that none of these different strategies provides a complete and adequate basis for developing the tools that research psychologists need in order to obtain a better understanding of personality or the tools that applied psychologists need in order to deal with the practical problems confronting them in industry, schools, and clinics. Only by using each of these strategies at appropriate but different stages in the development of assessment devices is it possible for us to avoid the limitations of each strategy and to develop assessment instruments which both further the understanding of personality and permit the accurate prediction of important behaviors.

Although the assessment of one person by another begins in early childhood, and although assessment procedures of a primitive variety are used daily by laymen in all walks of life, such lay assessments of persons are, in the light of present knowledge, often notoriously lacking in precision and/or fidelity. Only within the last fifty years have appropriate techniques been developed for evaluating the quality of assessments. These evaluative techniques, involving a combination of logic and statistics, now constitute a special branch of psychology known as *psychometrics*. Although much of psychometrics involves considerable understanding of statistical methods, certain of the more critical issues in the construction and evaluation of assessment devices can be readily appreciated without statistical sophistication. The most important of these methodological issues are the interrelated questions of the reliability and the validity of measures or scores resulting from the use of any assessment procedure.

RELIABILITY

In the simplest terms, the reliability of any measuring device refers to the precision with which it measures whatever it measures. To take an example from the domain of instruments designed to measure physical dimensions, it is obvious that some scales provide more precise measures of weight than do others; some are constructed to provide accuracy to the ounce, others only to the pound. Bathroom scales, for example, are usually labeled "Not legal for use in trade," and a customer might quite properly object to their use by his butcher!

As the result of scientific knowledge and improved technology, instruments for the measurement of physical dimensions such as length, weight, temperature, and pressure can now be constructed with almost any desired degree of precision, if one is simply willing to pay the price. But even in this realm of measurement, one is frequently content to use an instrument of less than near perfect accuracy, depending on the purpose for which the instrument is used. Thus, a cloth tape measure is sufficiently reliable for fitting a man's suit but not for building a complex machine from steel components.

When we turn to the realm of psychological measurement, the matter of precision is equally relevant, but the methodological problems of how to evaluate it are far more complicated. In the case of physical measuring instruments, we can always check the accuracy of a measure on an instrument in question by comparing it with that from a more elaborate (and usually more costly) instrument. Similar accepted standards of measurement are simply not available to the assessment psychologist. Nor, in most instances, as we have already noted, do the readings (or "scores") derived from assessment devices correspond to ratio scales. This means that one doesn't even dare to assume that a reading of "0" corresponds to "none" of whatever it is he is measuring.

How, then, does the psychometrician go about determining the precision or reliability of a set of measures? Recall that a trait is conceptualized as a continuum, and that each person can be thought of as being indicated by a certain point on this continuum. The reliability of a measure refers to the accuracy with which a person's score falls at the correct position on the continuum. To the degree that a test yields less than completely reliable scores, a person's score must be considered an approximation to his correct or "true score." However, since we have no standard instrument with which to determine his "true score," we have no direct way of ascertaining the degree to which a score is in error.

Confronted with this perplexing problem, the psychometrician tries to find the magnitude of error in psychological measurements in an indirect fashion; he asks "With what degree of consistency will a test order persons on a trait continuum?" A number of alternate operational procedures have been developed for answering this question. The result is that one may obtain not one but several different estimates of reliability depending on the nature of the operations and the assumptions involved. It is useful to consider three kinds of reliability.

RETEST RELIABILITY (STABILITY)

This estimate of reliability is established by administering the same test to the same group of persons on two different occasions and noting the degree to which persons are consistently located on the trait continuum. More specifically, reliability is the correlation (r_{tt}) between the two resulting sets of test scores. A perfectly reliable test, one with no errors of measurement, would result in a correlation (reliability coefficient) of $+1.00$. A completely unreliable test, i.e., one for which the scores are determined entirely by chance (and hence are all error) would result in a reliability coefficient of .00.

A reliability estimate based on two successive administrations of the same test is appropriate only if two assumptions are met: (1) that persons do not change their relative true positions on the trait continuum from the first to the second testing, and (2) that a person's experience in taking the test does not result in the test becoming, for him, on the second administration a different test. For certain types of assessment devices, these appear to be reasonable assumptions, especially if the intervening time interval is short. For other instruments, however, these assumptions are probably not justified and to the degree which they are not, the resulting reliability coefficient will be too low.

Even if persons do change their true relative positions on the trait continuum between the first and second administrations of the test, the coefficient of correlation between the two sets of scores may still be of interest but the degree to which it fails to approach $+1.00$ is an unknown function of (1) lack of precision of the assessment device *and* (2) the lack of stability of persons with respect to the trait being measured. For this reason, Cronbach (Cronbach, 1960) has appropriately proposed that any estimate of reliability based on two separate administrations of the same test be labeled *Coefficient of Stability*.

ALTERNATE-FORM RELIABILITY (EQUIVALENCE)

The alternate-form reliability estimate is also based on a comparison of (i.e., the correlation between) two sets of scores for the same persons, but is obtained by the administration of two *equivalent forms* of the same test— that is, two tests which presumably measure the same trait, but are composed of different questions or items. Unlike the manufacturer of thermometers, the developer of a new psychological assessment device is rarely in a position to make thousands of "equivalent forms" of his instrument, but he is sometimes successful in developing two or even three such alternate forms—different sets of test items which presumably assess the same variable or variables. In such instances, if two equivalent forms are administered with a relatively brief intervening time interval, one may evaluate the test's reliability by comparing the two sets of measures. The correlation of the two sets of scores provides another estimate of their reliability. To the degree that the two forms are not truly equivalent, the computed coefficient of reliability will again be too low but it is a very useful estimate of the lower bounds of the reliability of the measures. To distinguish this estimate of reliability from an estimate based on two administrations of the same test, Cronbach has proposed that a reliability-coefficient estimate from alternate forms of a test be called a *coefficient of equivalence*.

INTERNAL-CONSISTENCY RELIABILITY (HOMOGENEITY)

Even though one has but a single set of scores, based on but one administration of a test, it is still possible to estimate the reliability of such scores with considerable accuracy. The simplest procedure for carrying out this apparently impossible operation again consists of utilizing two scores for each person, each score based on random halves of the total test. One method for obtaining two presumably equivalent scores for each person is that of treating the odd and the even numbered items of a test as two "equivalent forms" and computing separate "odd" and "even" scores for each person. To the degree that these two sets of resulting scores agree (i.e., correlate highly) the scores on each half of the test may be assumed to be reliable or dependable. Because, in general, the longer the test the more reliable it is, the coefficient of correlation based on scores of a half test will be an underestimate of the reliability of scores based on the whole test. Fortunately, there is a simple formula for estimating the reliability of a test twice (or n times) as long, and hence it is possible to make reasonably accurate estimates of the reliability of scores based on the total test.

Other and better methods are available for estimating the reliability of scores obtained from a single administration of a test, but all, in one way or another, are estimates of the *homogeneity* of the scores, that is, the extent to which the instrument is measuring a relatively pure psychological continuum or variable. For this reason, reliability estimates based on a single set of scores are not appropriate for certain assessment devices (for example, some aptitude tests) which are intentionally designed to measure a combination of several different abilities or traits. Such heterogeneous tests may have considerable utility in practical assessment situations, but the reliability of the measures which they yield must be evaluated by either the retest or alternate-form methods discussed above.

Summarizing, reliability is an extremely important characteristic of any assessment technique. Only to the extent that one can expect scores to locate persons somewhere near their true positions on a trait continuum can one rely on the accuracy of the scores. In the absence of true scores, we must estimate the reliability of obtained scores by determining how consistently the scores differentiate among persons and order them on the continuum. Regardless of the method used, the resulting estimate of reliability is expressed as a coefficient of reliability (r_{tt}) ranging from .00 to $+ 1.00$.

The coefficient of correlation used in estimating reliability is a nonlinear trigonometric function (not an equal-interval scale) and therefore, it is not as readily interpreted as one might wish for such an important property of a set of measures. Furthermore, all estimates of reliability are markedly influenced by the range of the psychological variable in the sample of persons on which the coefficient is computed. This can be readily understood in terms of an illustration. Suppose one administers a test of intelligence on two occasions to a group of 30 eighth-grade students, including some who are so dull that they have scarcely been able to remain in public school and others so brilliant that they will go on to college and to graduate and professional schools.

Because of the wide *range of talent*, a relatively brief intelligence test might very well order these 30 students consistently on the two occasions and result in a relatively high coefficient of reliability (or stability). Suppose, however, we administer the same test on two occasions to another group of students, but that this second group is composed of 30 students, each of whom had received the highest overall grade record in some junior high school in a large city. Obviously, this second group will have a much narrower range of talent, and it is quite likely that a coefficient of reliability computed on the basis of the scores of this selected sample of able students will be much lower than that found for the group of students with the wide range of ability.

Because it is not expressed on a linear scale (i.e., one with equal intervals) and because it is markedly influenced by the range of talent of the persons tested, the coefficient of reliability is not the most useful index for communicating the level of precision or accuracy of a set of obtained scores. A much more meaningful statistic is available: the "Standard Error of Measure" (SE_M). The SE_M is simply an estimate of the probability of the difference between a person's obtained score and his "true" score. More specifically, the chances are 2 out of 3 that a person's true score is within ± 1 SE_M of his obtained score and about 95 chances in 100 that his true score is within ± 2 SE_M of his obtained score. There are still 5 chances in 100 that a person's obtained score is more than ± 2 SE_M away from his true score.

Since the SE_M varies widely from one test or assessment technique to another, depending not only on r_{tt} but also on the units in which the test is scored, one cannot judge whether a given SE_M is large or small merely by knowing its absolute size. It is more useful to know its size relative to what it would be if the test had no reliability whatsoever, that is, the SE_M of a set of scores obtained by estimating everyone's score at the average for the group. Fortunately, there is a well-known functional relationship between the SE_M and the coefficient of reliability (r_{tt}). It is:

$$SE_M = SD \sqrt{1 - r_{tt}}$$

where: SD is the standard deviation[1] of the obtained scores for a group of subjects and r_{tt} is the reliability coefficient. Note that if $r_{tt} = .00$, the SE_M is at a maximum and equal to the SD, in other words, as large as it would be if scores on the test were entirely the result of chance.

---

[1] In case the reader has not studied statistics, the SD is a measure of the variability or "spread" of any set of measures about their average value. For most sets of test scores, the SD is about $\frac{1}{5}$ or $\frac{1}{6}$ of the range between the highest and lowest score.

At the other extreme, if r_{tt} is 1.00, then SE_M is zero, meaning that there is no error in estimating true scores from obtained scores. The coefficient of reliability, r_{tt}, must be .75 before the SE_M is reduced to half its chance value, and even with a reliability of .91, the SE_M is still 30 percent of the amount it would be if the instrument were totally lacking in reliability. Unfortunately, but a relatively small proportion of all available assessment devices yield scores for which r_{tt} is as high as .90.

Lest the reader be troubled about the concept of a "true score," admittedly an abstraction, it may be helpful to think of ways of approximating such a score. Consider the measurement of simple reaction time of a student who is seated before a panel and told that as soon as he sees a light, he is to press a key. An electric timer permits a direct reading of the time that elapses between the flash of the bulb and the reaction. Presumably, there is some "true value" for the subject's reaction time, but his "obtained score" on any single trial is not likely to correspond exactly to this true value. On some trials he will react more quickly and on others less quickly, depending on a number of conditions both external and within the subject. In other words, his score for any one trial is likely to be in error by some amount.

Conceptually, the S's true score is the mean of a very large number of such obtained scores—assuming, of course, that the experiment has been conducted in a manner that eliminates the effects of boredom, fatigue, etc. Furthermore, the standard deviation of the distribution of a large number of such obtained scores around their average value corresponds to the standard error of measurement obtained by using the formula given above. This is helpful since it is ordinarily not feasible to test a subject repeatedly with the same test, and, for most tests, there is only one or at the most two or three forms available.

Before leaving the important topic of reliability, it is important to note that the concepts and methods which have been discussed largely within the framework of test scores are equally applicable to any kind of measurement or assessment. The methods described here are rarely used in the physical sciences, largely because technological advances in instrumentation permit measurement with such high levels of precision that the resulting r_{tt} values would approach 1.00 and SE_M values would approach .00. In general, physical scientists are in the enviable position of being able to measure almost any variable with any required degree of precision. When we turn to the biological sciences, however, the reliability of measurements becomes a critical problem. Suppose, for example, one wishes to measure the blood pressure of a human patient. Even though a physician is dealing with an easily defined variable and has a carefully calibrated physical instrument, a manometer, from which to read "the score," the consistency of repeated blood pressure measurements is far from perfect; in fact, the resulting coefficient of correlation between two sets of such measurements is typically no higher than that found for psychological tests. The errors of measurement of blood pressure are in part due to variations in the placement of the cuff on the arm and in part a function of external and internal conditions affecting the subject on any two occasions. And, if the two sets of measurements are made by two different physicians, they may vary even more because of differences in the criteria used by each in deciding at what manometer reading the pulse can no longer be heard through the stethoscope.

In the absence of suitable instruments, tests, or techniques, the assessment of many personal characteristics must rely on human judges who observe the behavior of an individual either on the job or in an interview and then make judgments on one or more of a wide array of psychological variables. If these judgments are quantified either by ranking or by the use of a rating scale, it is both feasible and desirable to ascertain the reliability of the resulting "scores." Fortunately, all of the methods of reliability estimation are directly appplicable to assessments in which human beings rather than instruments or tests constitute the primary assessment device. If the same judge ranks or rates a group of persons on two occasions, we can compute the counterpart of retest reliability. If two different persons judge the same subjects on the same occasion, we can compute the counterpart of alternate-form reliability. Using either of these reliability coefficients and the SD of the ratings, it is then possible to estimate the standard error of the obtained ratings (SE_M) just as if they were scores on a standardized test.

Finally, it is important to note that any set of fallible scores (those containing errors), such as those we must deal with in the behavioral sciences, will correlate higher with true scores than they will with another set of fallible scores. Intuitively, it would seem that no set of measures could correlate higher with anything else than they correlate with themselves, i.e., in a repeated set of measures. That such is possible is readily seen from the following example: Suppose that two persons, Judges A and B, are each asked to estimate the weight of 100 men. The correlation between the two resulting sets of fallible estimates would constitute an alternate-form estimate of reliability, r_{tt}. Suppose, however, by using a bathroom scale, we get another set of measures which more closely approximate the true weights of each of the 100 men. We would then be in a position to compute three coefficients of correlation:

Judge A's estimates and Judge B's estimates (r_{AB})
Judge A's estimates and scale weights (r_{AS})
Judge B's estimates and scale weights (r_{BS})

Since it is highly unlikely that the errors in the weights as estimated by Judge A will be the same as those in the weights as estimated by Judge B, and since the scale readings may be assumed to have relatively small errors, it is not surprising to find that both Judge A's and Judge B's estimates of weights correlate higher with the more nearly true weights than they do with each other.

In general, the correlation of any set of fallible scores with their corresponding true scores tends to be higher than their reliability (r_{tt}). The general relationship of these two correlations is simply

$$r_{\infty t} = \sqrt{r_{tt}}.$$

The *index of reliability*, $r_{\infty t}$, is the estimated correlation between a set of fallible scores and the corresponding set of true scores. As seen, it is simply the square root of the coefficient of reliability; since it is the square root of a decimal less than 1.00, it is always higher than the coefficient of reliability. The index of reliability is our best estimate of the degree to which any set of measures correspond to the presumed true measures of the phenomenon or person being assessed.

As we have noted, the reliability of any set of measures may be estimated by one or more alternate methods. But since any computed reliability coefficient is a function of (1) the instrument (test or technique), (2) the user of the instrument, (3) the conditions under which it is used, and (4) the range or variability of the trait represented in persons assessed, it is obvious that any estimate of reliability is a characteristic not of a test or technique but of a set of measures or scores resulting from a combination of (1), (2), (3), and (4). It is, therefore, never appropriate to ask about or discuss the reliability of any particular instrument, test, technique, or human judge without specifying the other potential sources of errors in the obtained measures. Instead, one should refer to the reliability of the measures obtained using a given instrument under specified conditions. And, a test which yields two or more scores, as is true for many assessment devices, has as many different reliabilities as the number of scores derived.

SOURCES OF UNRELIABILITY

From the attention that has been given to the topic of reliability, it may be assumed that the lack of reliability is a serious problem in psychological assessment. This is all too true. Reliability coefficients of .95 and over are almost nonexistent; those between .90 and .95 are rare; many of the best and more widely used tests have reliability coefficients between .70 and .90. Remember that with a reliability coefficient of .75, the standard error of measurement is still half as large as if all persons were not measured at all but simply assigned an average score on the test! The typical teacher-made objective test (true-false or multiple choice) is likely to yield scores with reliabilities ranging from .30 to .60, depending on the length of the test and the care that has gone into its construction. And, the typical teacher-made and graded essay test has been repeatedly shown to yield even lower reliabilities!

Why is it so difficult to measure psychological traits with precision? There are many reasons, the chief being that the behavior of the human organism is influenced by many variables in addition to the one which the test is designed to measure: moment-to-moment or day-to-day fluctuations in attention, motivation, state of health, fatigue, distraction, emotional states, etc. The result is that even for such a presumably narrow trait as simple reaction time, there is considerable variability in a subject's performance from trial to trial—so great that reliable measures can be obtained only by averaging measures over many trials for each person. In general, the more trials (i.e., the longer the test) the more reliable are the resulting means. When we move to slightly broader traits such as "ability to add," test behavior is still subject to all of the above mentioned extraneous influences, *and* we are also confronted with the fact that, because of learning and remembering, one cannot increase the length of the test merely by asking the subject to add the same numbers time after time. Instead, it is necessary to construct many different problems, all presumably measuring the same ability but differing in content. To the extent that the test constructor is successful in this effort, he can develop a test for which the total score, like the average of many reaction times, is a relatively accurate measure of "adding ability." And, to the extent the test problems are homogeneous, the scores will have a high coefficient of internal consistency. If there are too few samples of behavior (problems, items, etc.) the possible effect of extraneous variables is likely to result in extremely unreliable scores.

As we move to traits which are still more broadly conceptualized, e.g., reasoning ability, intelligence, creativity, anxiety, or rigidity, it becomes even more difficult to create enough different test questions or items of equivalent relevance to the trait to provide a reliable index of the core variable one seeks to measure. The result is that, as of today, many of the variables which are considered by some theorists to be key constructs in personality theory must be assessed by techniques which yield very imprecise measures or scores.

VALIDITY

As contrasted with reliability—which refers to the accuracy or the precision of the scores derived from any kind of an assessment technique, i.e., how correctly the scores order persons on whatever continuum the scores measure—validity refers to the question of *what the scores measure,* i.e., what they mean. As in the case of reliability, one properly speaks not of the validity of the test or technique but about the validity of each of the measures or scores provided by the technique.

Expressed in another way, the validity of a set of scores refers to the correctness of the inferences which one makes on the basis of the scores. Viewed in this light, a test has not only as many validities as scores but as many validities as different inferences based on its scores! Certain of these inferences may be appropriate or highly valid, and other inferences based on the same scores or sets of scores may be unwarranted, or lacking in validity.

Let us again use an illustration from the domain of physical measurement. The familiar yardstick yields reasonably reliable measures, whether used on two occasions by one person or used by more than one person. Therefore, we can have considerable confidence in the accuracy of the measures it yields—*as long as we use it to measure the distance between two points.* Thus one can use it to measure the length of tables, the height of persons, or the depth of water at various points in a stream. However, suppose someone told us that he had measured the rates of flow of water in several streams merely by sticking the yardstick down against the bottom and reading off the "scores" where the surface of the water met the yardstick. Intuitively, we would reject these scores as invalid measures of "rate of flow." They might be highly accurate and reliable measures of something, in this case, depth, but not valid measures of rate of flow.

When we move from the domain of physical to psychological measurement, the issue of validity is much more complex. Our hypothetical constructs are not nearly so well defined as those in the physical sciences; our theories are not as rigorous, and there is much less consensus regarding the appropriateness of specified operations for the measurement of variables. The result is that, as we noted before, two tests purporting to measure the *same* psychological trait may yield scores which do not correlate at all—or, conversely, two tests purporting to measure *different* traits may yield scores which correlate so highly that they force the conclusion that they are in fact measuring the same trait under different labels. Such disconcerting findings have led psychologists during the last 20 years to systematic analyses of the problems of validity and to several methodological innovations in evaluating this crucially important aspect of assessment devices. At this point it is useful to delineate several alternative conceptions of validity and to note certain implications of each for different kinds of assessment devices (see also Hays,1967b; and "Standards for Evaluating Educational and Psychological Tests and Manuals," 1967).

CONSENSUAL VALIDITY

Since validity in its broadest sense is concerned with meaning, it is not surprising that one approach to the problem is that of securing the agreement of experts as to the meaning of the measures derived from a particular test. This approach to the problem of validity is most often used in the construction of tests of educational achievement and in the interpretation of the scores based on them. Suppose a teacher of history wished to construct a test to measure knowledge of, or achievement in, American history. While he might, if he were cocksure, rely entirely on his own opinion as to what does and does not constitute the subject matter of American history, he would be well advised to at least check his opinions against a sample of widely used textbooks in American history and to limit the questions which he included to facts and principles included in two or more of the texts. In so doing, he would be more likely to produce a test that would be accepted by his fellow historians as measuring achievement in American history. Even so, he might find his colleagues unwilling to accept his decisions as to how to weight certain topics.

In order to achieve an even greater degree of consensual validity in the construction of achievement tests, test producers, such as the Educational Testing Service, have found it essential to employ a panel of expert consultants to arrive at specifications regarding the definition of the field and the relative weight to be given to each of the subareas and topics. Such a panel may write the test items or be asked to review them critically after they have been written by others. In this manner, it is possible to produce a test which most knowledgeable people will agree measures achievement in any specified school subject. Such tests are said to have *consensual validity* because experts agree that they measure what they purport to measure.

Why should a similar procedure not be satisfactory in developing measures of other psychological variables—such as aptitudes, attitudes, or values? Simply because there is a marked lack of consensus among presumed experts regarding the meanings of the words used and the appropriateness of inferring a person's position on any given trait continuum from particular types of assessment data, whether of the L, Q, or T varieties.

Perhaps the closest approach to the use of consensual validity in the construction of tests other than in the field of educational achievement occurs when the test developer asks his colleagues (or even his graduate students) to judge a set of test items—first, as to whether or not they are relevant to the assessment of some trait, let's say anxiety, and to indicate which of two or more alternative responses should be scored as indicating a more anxious person. Such *a priori* decisions regarding the appropriateness of inferences from behavior to position on a trait continuum are of course characteristic of the rational strategies discussed in the previous chapter. A certain degree of consensus may be reached by a test developer and his immediate associates regarding the nature of the behaviors to be sampled and the weights to be assigned in scoring for a given trait; while a number of widely used tests have been constructed in this fashion, the degree of consensus among psychologists is simply not sufficient for such instruments to be generally accepted as "valid."

Worse still, two different groups of investigators, seeking to measure the same trait, may (1) agree among themselves regarding both the behavior to be sampled and the method of scoring, (2) end up with entirely different tests, and (3) learn later that there is no agreement in the manner in which persons are ordered on the trait continuum by the two tests! As an example of such an unfortunate outcome, consider two techniques of assessing "need achievement," both based on Murray's theory of human needs (1938). The first was developed by McClelland and Atkinson (1953) and requires that subjects tell brief stories in response to selected TAT pictures. The resulting stories are then scored in terms of the apparent number and strength of achievement—related needs contained in the stories. The second measure of need achievement is derived from the Edwards Personal Preference Schedule (1954), in which the subject is presented with a large number of paired statements and is instructed to choose the one of each pair that is most true for him. Certain of these choices are presumed to be indicative of need achievement and one's score on need achievement is simply the sum of these choices. In a few studies where the same persons have been assessed with both of these purported measures of need achievement, the resulting correlations between the two measures have been near zero. Obviously, these two tests are not measuring the same variables. This example indicates the problem of achieving consensual validity among psychologists as to what a given personality test measures.

EMPIRICAL VALIDITY

A very different approach to the meaning of a set of test scores involves asking how useful the scores are in telling us something about the person's day-to-day behavior. For example, do the scores enable us to *discriminate* normals from psychotics, alcoholics from nonalcoholics, or to *predict* future performance of persons on such criteria as performance in college, in pilot training, in life-insurance sales, or the adjustment of prisoners released on parole? It is useful to differentiate between two kinds of practical or empirical validity.

CONCURRENT VALIDITY

A set of test scores are said to have concurrent validity to the extent that they discriminate two (or more) groups of persons already known to be different, on the basis of other evidence. One may ask, why, if the groups are already known to be different, should one wish to differentiate them by test scores? There are three reasons:

1. It is possible that the test scores may provide a more economical basis for categorization than methods previously employed for the same purpose.

2. To the degree that the test scores differentiate groups known to differ in present performance or social adjustment, it is likely (although not necessary) that their scores will also be useful in predicting the future behavior of persons not yet differentiated by their life behavior.

3. To the extent that anything is known about the ways in which the criterion groups differ from each other, we have a possible basis for making inferences regarding the trait(s) being assessed by the test.

PREDICTIVE VALIDITY

A set of assessments (test scores, ratings, etc.) are said to have predictive validity to the extent that they are useful in predicting the actual performance of persons in the *future*. Conceptually, this is very much like concurrent validity except for the time dimension. But, from the standpoint of practical value, this distinction is very important. An assessment device which has concurrent validity for differentiating between groups known to differ may also have predictive validity for predicting future behavior, but such is not necessarily the case. Consider, for instance, the possible differences between a group of penitentiary inmates and a group of law-abiding men matched for age, education, and social status. It is very probable that one could devise an assessment device that would discriminate these groups very well even though it measures only the effects of long-term institutionalization. While such an assessment device would be of great interest to an investigator studying the effects of institutionalization, it might prove to be completely worthless as a predictor of future criminal behavior.

Psychologists primarily concerned with the construction of empirically valid assessment techniques typically rely on the rational strategy for deciding what kinds of assessment data shall be collected but utilize the empirical strategy to decide how test behaviors should be scored to predict the criterion in which they are interested. In other words, inferences from assessment data to actual behavior are made only to the degree that research has demonstrated sufficiently high correlations to justify them. While both theory and a rational analysis may guide the psychologist in the early stages of developing such an assessment device, the eventual decision to retain a test item is made on a very pragmatic basis: "Does it work—i.e., does this test response contribute to better discrimination of groups or to the more accurate prediction of behavior in the real-life situation?"

Since performance in most situations is determined not by one but a combination of several conceptually different psychological traits, tests devised to have the best predictive validity are usually heterogeneous, i.e., typically involve the simultaneous assessment of two or even several traits. For this reason such tests are of relatively little interest to psychologists whose primary interest is in personality theory or other fields of psychology where there is a need for relatively pure measures of homogeneous traits.

CONSTRUCT VALIDITY

A construct is a hypothetical variable which some theorist has proposed as necessary (or at least useful) in explaining the relationships among phenomena in the domain with which the theory is concerned. It is always an inferred "thing" and is always designated by a noun. Many named traits (abilities, needs, etc.) are essential constructs in some psychological theory of personality.

The construct validity of any measure refers to the degree to which the measure, in fact, provides an appropriate basis for making inferences regarding the construct it purports to measure. Whereas it is a relatively simple matter to determine whether or not, and how well, a "sales-aptitude test" predicts actual selling performance, it is an extremely long and involved matter to ascertain the degree to which a purported measure of "anxiety" in fact measures anxiety. In the absence of external criteria for the presence or absence of or the amount of anxiety which a person possesses, it is simply not possible to design any single experiment to evaluate the amount of construct validity possessed by any set of presumed measures of anxiety. One can develop confidence in the value of any construct and in the construct validity of a set of measures only as the result of a series of experiments in which it is found that persons who score "high" on a test behave differently from persons who score "low" and that this difference is *in accord with theoretical predictions*.

Most present day personality theories are so nonrigorous in the definitions of their constructs and in their explication of necessary relationships among them that there is as yet tragically little consensus regarding either key trait constructs or the best methods of assessing them. Instead, we find, as has already been noted, the confusing situation whereby Investigators A and B may each develop (and even market!) a purported test of Construct X, but subsequent application of the two tests to the same group reveals no more than chance relationships between the two sets of measures. Obviously, both tests cannot have construct validity for the same construct. For scientists, such a finding points to one of three possible conclusions:

1. A's test measures Construct X, or
2. B's test measures Construct X, or
3. Neither test measures Construct X.

Only through further investigations to determine the relationships of both sets of scores to a wide variety of behaviors is it possible to choose between these three mutually exclusive possibilities.

Alternatively, as we have also noted, two assessment techniques may purport to measure different constructs, yet the measures which they yield correlate as highly as the reliabilities of the two sets of scores will permit. Confronted with this unfortunate and all too common situation, the scientist has a choice of two conclusions:

1. Construct X is the same as Construct Y, in spite of the fact that the two bear a different label and may have a different theoretical basis, or
2. Both techniques are measuring the same construct, but perhaps a different one, Construct Z!

Again, the choice between these alternative conclusions must await the accumulation of further research evidence. In the long run, the question "What does a test measure?" must be answered in terms of a continuing analysis of the correlations of its scores with as many other different measures and criteria as possible. Each such newly discovered relationship is potentially helpful in sharpening the *true* meaning of any set of test scores—in other words, their construct ability.

IN CONCLUSION

Regardless of which of the three kinds of reliability we may consider, all are in one way or another an index of the consistency of the kind of behavior sampled. Because of the number and variety of conditions which may influence a specific piece of human behavior (i.e., a response to a single situation) it is not surprising that the most common basis for low reliability of a set of test scores is that they are based on too few samples of behavior. Just as a single reaction time may be longer or shorter than a subject's typical reaction time, a certain test question may be very easy for one student and difficult for another. In general, the more samples of behavior obtained, the more stable is the total or average score. Other things being equal, longer tests involving more questions tend to yield more reliable scores than shorter ones involving fewer questions.

In turn, the lack of reliability of a set of test scores places a very definite ceiling on their validity, whether we are interested in the concurrent, predictive, or construct validity of the scores. Since, as we have noted, the index of reliability

$$\sqrt{r_{tt}}$$

is an estimate of the correlation of a set of obtained scores with corresponding true scores, it is obvious that the scores cannot possibly correlate any higher with any other kind of behavior. Thus a set of scores with a reliability of .81 could conceivably predict some real-life criterion performance with a validity coefficient of .90. By contrast, a set of scores which are so lacking in consistency that they will correlate with themselves only .25 cannot possibly predict any other behavior with a validity coefficient of more than .50. And, these are top limits! In actual practice, it is most unusual for a set of test scores to agree with criterion measures (i.e., nontest behavior) as closely as they do with themselves.

The usefulness of any assessment technique is obviously a function of both the reliability and the validity of the measures which it provides. Unless these measures have some reliability, they are of no more use than if they had been assigned by a toss of dice or some other game of chance. And, in general, the more reliable the measures—the more accurate they are—the greater the potential value of the technique for both research and practice. But reliability alone is not enough. No matter how great the precision of a set of measures, their scientific worth and/or their practical utility is always a function of the degree to which they are demonstrably related to "something" other than themselves. This "something" may be other key variables posited in a theoretical system; it may be a socially important set of categories of persons in a society; or it may be the performance of persons in any one of a wide array of situations.

From the preceding discussion of reliability and validity, it should be evident that it makes no logical sense whatsoever to ask the general questions "How reliable or valid is Technique A?—is it more reliable or valid than Test B?" First of all, as we have noted, there are several alternate ways of defining both reliability and validity. These alternate definitions are each logically defensible, but they are not equivalent. Secondly, none of the operations involved in determining any of the varieties of either reliability or validity is based on the instrument itself but rather on measures or scores obtained by applying the instrument to a group of persons. Thirdly, since many assessment techniques yield several different scores or indices, it is probable that each of the scores will be found to have different reliabilities and validities. Finally, even a single score from a test will have as many different validities as the number of different inferences which are made from the score.

Thus, one may find that for a single set of scores, the reliability is low if computed as internal consistency but high when computed on a retest basis. The concurrent validity of the same scores may be high for differentiating National Merit Scholars and school dropouts, but low for differentiating groups majoring in science from those majoring in the humanities. The same scores may show a high predictive validity for one type of performance and none for another. In addition, the scores may readily be interpretable as defining a psychological construct or there may be no agreement whatsoever as to the psychological continuum being assessed. Finally, two sets of scores derived from the same instrument are likely to have a very different pattern of reliabilities and validities.

Long before he is able to use language, a child, like the lower animals, learns to discriminate among objects, plants, and other creatures. Presumably all of the order in man's conceptions of natural phenomena began with his perception of differences among the things surrounding him. The development of language has enabled the human species to make dramatic progress both in the number of such discriminations and in the transmission of them to succeeding generations.

The structure of language suggests that these discriminations are of three broad kinds: things (nouns), actions (verbs), and characteristics of things (adjectives). It is likely that all assessment and measurement began with the broad classification of real objects and their designation by nouns: rocks, food, water, animals, people, etc.; this was probably followed by the discrimination and labeling of such essential characteristics of the objects by adjectives: hard, wet, useful, friendly, etc. Only later, presumably, did man identify properties such as distance, hardness, temperature, and velocity with abstract nouns. Although we now have instruments which provide precise measures of the degree to which these physical properties are present, their crude "measurement" by human judges still suffices in some situations: a substance may be judged as "hard as a rock," the temperature of water as "near freezing," or the velocity of the wind as "strong."

The richness of all languages in words used to describe perceived differences among people makes it plain that assessment of man by his fellow man has been going on for a long time. Furthermore, human judgment is still by all odds the most widely used assessment technique, if we include lay as well as professional assessments. Such assessments, typically expressed in the form of adjectives (handsome, bright, boring, honest), are apparently adequate for much social interaction. However, such unsystematic forms of assessment do not readily permit the comparison of two different persons, or the ordering of several persons on any trait continuum.

When a human judge is asked to compare Person A with Person B on any given characteristic, e.g., intelligence, he may judge A as "brighter," as "equal to," or as "duller" than B. If the judge categorizes all people as either bright or dull, he has established a crude scale that provides for only two levels of discrimination. If the judge is willing to introduce a middle category of persons, who, in his judgment, are neither bright nor dull, we have a scale with a little greater potential precision. If the judge believes he can discriminate as many as 5 or 7 levels of "intelligence," we have the possibility of ordering persons on a 5-point or a 7-point continuum.

Because most assessment techniques rely heavily on the judgments of human beings, either in the original construction of the technique, or in daily use, psychologists have devoted much effort to the development of systematic procedures for collecting human judgments in ways which enhance their value in communication and permit their statistical analysis. Instruments used to collect and record systematic judgments are called rating scales.

TYPES OF RATING SCALES

The *numerical* rating scale is one that divides a trait continuum into several gradations; the rater is merely asked to indicate his judgment by encircling a number. Thus, for the trait of intelligence, a simple scale might be:

> 5—Brilliant
> 4—Above average
> 3—Average
> 2—Below average
> 1—Dull

In the case of *graphic* rating scales, the trait continuum is indicated by a line (either vertical or horizontal). The trait continuum may be designated simply by a noun (e.g., intelligence), by the use of adjectives at each end (e.g., brilliant-dull), or it may include several adjectives or phrases to serve as "landmarks" or reference points along the scale. The judge merely makes a check mark at that point on the line which in his judgment is most descriptive of each subject. These judgments are then transformed to ratings by use of an arbitrary numerical scale.

The *adjective checklist* rating scale consists of a standard list containing a large number (e.g., 300) adjectives or descriptive phrases. Such a checklist may be used with a variety of different instructions, such as: "check only those which you believe to be most descriptive of the person;" "check the 20 which you believe to be most descriptive;" "check the 20 most descriptive and the 20 least descriptive of the person."

A variation of the checklist type of rating scale widely used since World War II is the so-called *Q Sort*. Here the rater is given a stack of cards (e.g., 76) on each of which is printed an adjective or descriptive phrase. He is told to sort these cards so that a specified number (usually an odd number, 5 or 7) of cards are in each of several categories ranging from a category labeled "least like" to one labeled "most like" the person being judged.

A variant of the adjective checklist is known as the *forced-choice rating scale*. Developed primarily because judges are typically loathe to rate their associates in an unfavorable portion of any continuum, the forced-choice procedure involves presenting the judge with groups of three or four adjectives of approximately equal social desirability and instructing him to mark the one adjective *most* and the one *least* descriptive of the person being rated.

Still another variety of rating scales for use with groups is that used to collect what are known as *sociometric* or *peer ratings*. Each member of a group, e.g., a class, or a Boy Scout troop, is asked to designate which one, two, or three persons in his group fall into certain categories indicated by questions such as:

"Whom do you like best? Least?"
"Whom would you most prefer as a camping companion? Least?"

The measure or score for each individual is derived merely by algebraically summing the number of positive and negative nominations received on each item. This procedure yields both positive and negative scores. Members not chosen by anyone in the most or least category would receive a score of "0" for that item.

THE BEHAVIORAL BASES OF JUDGMENTS

Most human beings are surprisingly willing to judge other persons with respect to many different characteristics on the basis of a remarkably small sample of behavior, for instance, a five minute conversation. While they may feel more comfortable with judgments based on a hour's interview, or behavior observed over an extended period of time (in school, or the job, or in social settings), some are also willing to make judgments about many traits on the basis of a relatively small sample of a behavioral product such as handwriting, a short story, a drawing, or even a photograph of the subject. Astrologers ask only that they be provided with the date (and perhaps the hour) of a subject's birth!

Literally hundreds of investigations have been conducted to determine the usefulness of judgments based on differing kinds and amounts of behavior and various behavioral products. Since all judgments (i.e., inferences from behavior to trait rating) are always made in the mind of an individual judge, the value of any set of ratings must be evaluated, first, with respect to the behavioral sample or behavioral product used as a basis for the judgment and, second, in terms of the behavior of the judges who make such inferences. We shall review first the evidence regarding the validity of assessments arrived at on the basis of different kinds of behavior.

SOMATIC CHARACTERISTICS

Among the earliest used methods of assessment are those which rely on an assumed relationship between physical (somatic) and psychological characteristics. *Phrenology*, for example, assumes a relationship between the shape of the head (its lumps and depressions) and some 30 personality traits. *Physiognomy* assumes a relationship between bodily features (e.g., shape of the jaw, chin, hands, or hair color) and personality. Whenever assessments based on such assumptions have been systematically evaluated, they have been regularly found to be completely lacking in validity.

Kretschmer's proposed physical types and Sheldon's proposed three dimensions of physique (endomorphic, mesomorphic, and ectomorphic) have fared but little better as a basis for assessing personality characteristics when their claims have been systematically evaluated by other investigators. Although available evidence indicates that there is probably some relationship between body build and a limited number of personality variables, such relationships are but weak ones. Even weak relationships are of considerable interest to scientists (e.g., there is a very slight positive correlation of height and intelligence), but when correlations are weak, they do not provide useful assessments of personality variables based on the physical characteristics.

Offhand, it would appear that physiological as contrasted with physical characteristics might serve as more appropriate bases for judging personality variables. Thus measures of heart rate, blood pressure, endocrine balance, brain waves (EEG's), muscular tension, and skin resistance have all been studied as potentially useful indicators of personality traits. Some of these physiological measures have been found to be systematically related to certain personality traits, but the correlations all tend to be low. Although slightly higher than those between physical characteristics and personality traits, they are still too low to justify the use of physiological measures in personality assessment. In part, the low validities obtained for physiological measures are due to the fact that the retest reliability of such measures tends to be low. For example, Wenger (1948) reports a coefficient of stability after 3 to 4 months of only .33 for both systolic and diastolic blood pressure.

STYLISTIC BEHAVIOR

There is a widespread belief that every individual reveals his true personality not only by what he does, but how he does it. Therefore, it is not surprising that many judges, in assessing the personality of another person, rely heavily on his characteristic postures, mannerisms, speech, and other so-called expressive forms of behavior. Does he typically stand erect or does he slouch? Is his handshake strong or limp? Does he speak loudly or softly? Does he gesture when speaking, and if so, what are his characteristic gestures?

Judgments based on these and similar aspects of expressive behavior have been studied by many investigators. In general, judges tend to agree fairly well in their ratings of traits based on experimentally isolated aspects of expressive behavior—voice recordings, silent movies, or walking—but the validity of such ratings tends to be low, that is, they do not agree with ratings of the same traits based on more varied samples of behavior. Of course, there are marked differences in styles of behavior displayed by individuals, and these may be well worth studying in their own right for the very reason that they so often influence the judgments of others. However, all available evidence makes it clear that one does not dare generalize very far in judging personality traits solely from the stylistic aspects of behavior.

BEHAVIORAL PRODUCTS

Certain aspects of behavioral style are embodied in the products of an individual's behavior: a short story, an autobiography, drawings, paintings, and handwriting. While almost any type of product may be and has been used as a basis for inferences about the personality of the individual who produced it, handwriting has probably been used longer and more frequently than any other. It is not surprising, therefore, that the claims of *graphology* have been the subject of many studies by psychologists. Persons claiming to be expert graphologists and students with no special training have both served as judges. In some studies, the task was simply that of identifying handwriting samples of persons falling in clearly distinguishable groups: men or women, criminals or noncriminals; in other studies, judges were asked to rate the individuals on one or more traits on the basis of a sample of their writing.

The findings of these studies may be summarized as follows: Both experts and nonexperts tend to show considerable agreement with each other with respect to judgments based on handwriting, but only slightly better than chance agreement with external criteria of the same characteristics. Although many graphologists insist that the sex of the writer is one of the most difficult traits to judge from handwriting, repeated studies show that it is the one most accurately judged—the proportion of correct judgments typically being between 60 and 70 percent. But, in spite of the claims made by adherents of graphology, it is now evident that a sample of handwriting, even when analyzed by experts, provides a very inadequate basis for inferences regarding personality traits.

A number of so-called "tests" using samples of expressive behavior have been developed and are currently used to provide bases for a variety of judgments regarding personality. These include: (1) the Bender-Gestalt, in which the subject is asked to copy several geometric figures of differing complexity, (2) the Mira Myokinetic Tests, in which the subject is blindfolded and instructed to draw ten lines of three kinds (straight, zig-zag, chains) on a blank piece of paper clipped to a board which is placed in three different positions—horizontal, vertical, and vertical-edgewise to the subject, (3) the HTP Test in which the subject is merely instructed to draw a picture of a person, a tree, and a house. In all instances, the inferences regarding the personality of the subject are based largely on theory or speculation. Users of these and similar techniques can learn to agree reasonably well in their judgments or interpretations of such products, but since inferences made are based largely on untested hypotheses, they have typically been found to have but little validity when checked against other assessments of the same personality traits.

SITUATION TESTS

"Situation test" is the term used to describe more or less structured situations in which a person (or small group of persons) is observed. Inferences are made about personality variables from behavior observed in these circumstances. One type of situation test involves instructing the subject to play a designated role. If two persons are observed at the same time, each may be instructed to interact with the other in specified roles and then perhaps to exchange their roles. In other types of situation tests, groups of subjects may be asked to discuss an assigned topic, to solve a problem, or to engage in a physical task requiring the co-operation of the group members. Situations may be made more or less stressful by the nature of the tasks or of the instructions, or by the use of a stooge or accomplice who, although ostensibly a member of the group, is actually a part of the "situation" with instructions to do everything he can to disrupt the smooth functioning of the individual or group in an assigned task.

Situation tests were extensively used in the OSS program (1948) and were used experimentally by Kelly and Fiske (1951). Available evidence indicates that (1) judges agree reasonably well with each other in evaluating personality traits from such miniature life situations, and (2) their ratings show some validity when checked against other measures of the same traits. However, the validities of ratings based on single situations or brief behavior samples tend to be very low. And, from the standpoint of efficiency, this method of assessment is relatively costly as regards the amount of professional time involved.

INTERVIEWS

The interview is one of the oldest and most frequently used situation tests. There are many kinds of interviews but all may be described as a face-to-face conversation between two persons, structured by one of them for a particular purpose. The purpose may be as varied as: to sell the subject an insurance policy, to evaluate him as a prospective student or employee, to provide information used in arriving at a diagnosis, or to help a patient to resolve an emotional problem. Even when used primarily as a basis for assessing personality characteristics, the nature of the interview varies greatly depending on the theoretical orientation and preferred practice of the interviewer. It may be so highly structured as to constitute essentially an orally administered questionnaire or so unstructured as "Tell me about yourself." Even though highly structured, interviews vary greatly with respect to content; i.e., the questions asked may concern facts regarding the subject's past experience; his present attitude toward a variety of persons, groups, or programs; or his hopes and aspirations for the future. They may be long or short, the interviewer may prefer to have familiarized himself with a wide range of information about the subject, or he may choose to interview the subject "cold." Interviews may be relaxed or stressful.

Regardless of their differences, all interviews share certain common characteristics which may be more determining of the interviewer's judgments than generally assumed. Regardless of the purpose or content of an interview, all provide the opportunity of observing the physical characteristics of the subject, his dress, his voice quality, and the stylistic or expressive aspects of his behavior, such as his posture, manner of speaking, his composure. It is probable that interviewers differ greatly with respect to the degree to which their judgments are influenced by such aspects of the interview situation as compared with the factual information obtained in the interview. Few, if any, interviewers really know how they weight data in arriving at personality assessments from an interview.

EXTENSIVE OBSERVATIONS OF BEHAVIOR

On the basis of all available evidence, the most dependable basis for judging the personality involves a great many samples of behavior, elicited in a wide variety of situations. Since it is rarely feasible or economical to collect the necessary number and varieties of behavioral samples in an arranged assessment situation, it is common practice to select as judges persons who have had the opportunity to observe a person over an extended period of time, e.g., teachers, supervisors, close colleagues, or fellow members of groups who have worked or played together for extended periods of time. Even these do not constitute "ideal judges" since each has typically had the opportunity to observe the person in but a limited variety of situtations. Judgments based on many observations of behavior in any of these three settings tend to be more valid than those based on more limited samples of behavior such as elicited by an interview, a single standardized test, or a situation test. But, because a person may in fact behave somewhat differently in school, on his job, or at play, even more valid assessments of him may be obtained by averaging the judgments of different persons who have had an opportunity to observe his behavior in each of these life roles.

LIMITATIONS OF JUDGES AND THEIR RATINGS

Although our present state of knowledge and technology requires that a large proportion of human assessment involve human judges who evaluate traits for which better measures are not yet available, all judges (and their ratings) are subject to such serious limitations that they must be used with full awareness of the errors that may result from their use. Judges are but human, and therefore likely to err in making inferences from behavior. Certain types of rating errors are so common that they have been named.

First, there are systematic biases of individual judges. The "leniency error" refers to the tendency of judges to rate others toward the favorable end of all trait continua. This tendency is especially marked when the judge is a close friend of the person rated or when the judge is aware that the ratings may be used to determine the person's opportunity for employment or promotion. Some harsh judges, however, tend to show the opposite bias in their ratings, that is, a proclivity to rate most subjects toward the unfavorable end of trait continua.

Another troublesome source of error in ratings is known as the "halo error." Consider the situation in which a judge has an adequate basis for judging one trait but is asked to rate a subject on several other traits for which he has no adequate basis to make a judgment. If the judge is reasonably sure that a person is very bright, he is likely to rate him as also very honest, very persevering, and high in initiative. This tendency to rate a person similarly on all traits results, of course, in positive correlations, even rather high ones, between the ratings of all pairs of traits, even though other measures of the same variables may show them to be essentially unrelated.

Another source of error in ratings is the tendency of many judges to see others as either very similar to, or as sharply contrasting to themselves. An example of the "similarity error" appears in a study by Landis (1936) who found that tall judges tend to overrate height, fat judges to overrate weight, and emotionally unstable judges to overrate instability in others. As an example of the "contrast error," talented judges tend to underestimate the same talent or skill of average subjects. Similarly, a judge who himself is always immaculately dressed might tend to underrate most of his associates on "neatness of dress."

Still other errors in rating result from the use of different definitions of traits by different raters and the use of differential weights which they assign to the behavioral indicators on which they rely as a basis for their judgments.

In view of these and still other sources of error in ratings, it is hardly surprising to find that there is typically but little agreement in the ratings of two judges on the same trait for the same persons, even though both use the same sample(s) of behavior as a basis for their rating. Fortunately, however, it appears that the errors of different judges are rather randomly distributed so that their errors of rating tend to cancel each other. Hence the average ratings of two judges tend to correlate higher with the average rating of two other judges than do the ratings of any one judge with those of any other judge. In general, just as longer tests with more questions or items tend to yield higher reliabilities and hence higher potential validities than shorter tests, the greater the number of judges whose ratings are averaged, the more stable and presumably the more valid is the resulting trait assessment.

For any trait, the correlation between the ratings of two judges or between the averages of ratings of groups of judges is an index which reflects both the reliability and one aspect of the validity of the ratings; to the extent that subjects are similarly ordered on the trait dimension, the ratings may be said to be reliable. But since any correlation reflects some agreement between judges with respect to the definition or meaning of the trait rated, the same correlation is also an index of consensual validity, i.e., interjudge agreement regarding the trait being rated. The extent to which the ratings of an individual judge or the pooled ratings of a group of judges have concurrent, predictive, or construct validity are questions that can be answered only by appropriately designed studies involving correlation of the ratings with other variables, e.g., diagnostic category, performance in training, on the job, or in appropriately planned experimental situations.

CONDITIONS ESSENTIAL FOR GOOD RATINGS

On the basis of what is now a very extensive body of evidence, a number of generalizations are possible regarding the reliability and validity of the ratings of human judges.

INCREASING INTERJUDGE AGREEMENT

In spite of their known fallibility, human judges tend to show some agreement in the assessment of a wide array of traits, i.e., the correlations are practically always positive. While a wide range of values has been reported, depending on the judges, the traits being rated, the basis of the ratings, etc., interjudge correlations of .50 can be achieved.

Interjudge agreement tends to be higher when the ratings are based on the same behavioral sample than when they are based on different samples of behavior. Thus, there is likely to be much more agreement between the ratings of two judges if the ratings are derived from the same set of TAT stories than if one judge bases his ratings on TAT stories and the other on an autobiography.

The level of interjudge agreement can be considerably increased by (1) the use of carefully designed rating forms and procedures, and (2) the training of judges with respect to trait definitions and the avoidance of the more common sources of rating error referred to above.

INCREASING THE VALIDITY OF RATINGS

While it is desirable that judges agree in their ratings, interjudge agreement is in itself a hollow accomplishment unless the ratings have some kind of validity; that is, the ratings must permit correct inferences about the behavior of persons in other situations. Thus, it is possible that although two judges trained in the same system of graphology may agree closely in evaluating intelligence from handwriting samples, their ratings will bear no relationship to intelligence as measured by any test or as reflected in school grades. The critical question is, "What are the conditions which increase the validity of ratings?" Available evidence warrants certain generalizations:

1. The validity of ratings is heavily dependent on the appropriateness of the behavior sample used as a basis for judgment. Thus observation of school children on the playground may permit extremely valid ratings of "activity level" or "aggressiveness" but completely invalid ratings of intelligence, curiosity, and a host of other traits. A child's handwriting may serve as an appropriate basis for judging "motor coordination" but not for judging "sociability." Regretfully, both laymen and professionals use a limited sample of behavior—limited in both kind and amount—to make unwarranted inferences regarding a wide array of traits for which the behavior sample is simply not relevant.

If a judge wishes to assess a subject with respect to a large number of traits, he requires not one but a relatively large number of samples of behavior of different kinds, in a variety of settings, and preferably over an extended period of time. Even so, the resulting ratings are those for but one judge, and, therefore, very fallible ones, i.e., of extremely limited reliability and therefore limited validity.

2. Since the errors of judgment of one judge are usually independent of the errors of judgment of a second judge, the average ratings of two judges tend to be typically both more reliable and more valid than those of a single judge. And, while the increase in validity is not linearly related to the number of judges whose ratings are averaged, it has been generally found that the greater the number of judges, the more reliable and valid are the averages of their ratings on practically all personality traits.

In research settings which permit the use of many professional staff members, it is entirely feasible to assign several judges to make ratings on the basis of a wide variety of behavioral samples. Thus, several judges may observe the same interview through a one-way mirror, listen to a recorded interview, observe the same behavior in situation tests, or analyze the same autobiography or TAT protocol, each making independent ratings of the same traits from the same behavioral samples. In some research programs, judges are asked to participate in a "staff conference" at which discrepancies in their independent ratings are discussed and an effort made to arrive at the best possible group rating Such conferences are likely to result in the judges being more confident of the validity of the group ratings, but available evidence indicates that they are typically no better than the simple averages of the independent ratings of the several judges. In a word, such staff conferences appear to be more satisfying to the judges than they are functional in contributing to better assessments.

In the practical world, there are certain realistic limitations on the number of judges that may be used to make ratings of the same people on the same traits from the same samples of behavior. Most persons find that there are but few others who have known them long enough and in enough varied situations to serve as good references. And, while it would be technically possible for an industry to use multiple interviewers, or multiple judges of the same recorded interview, such procedures for increasing the validity of judgments tend to be regarded as prohibitively costly in terms of professional time. The result is that the ratings of single judges, even though low in both reliability and validity, are widely used to arrive at decisions very importantly affecting the lives of individuals.

CATEGORIES OF JUDGES

In the preceding discussion we have used the term judge in its generic meaning to refer to a person making an evaluation of any characteristic on the basis of any kind of behavior or behavioral product. It is useful, however, to distinguish several categories of judges.

EXPERT JUDGES

Expert judges are persons who, by virtue of special training and/or experience, are presumed to be capable of making more valid inferences from specific types of assessment data than persons without special professional training in the use of a particular assessment technique. The number of different kinds of such alleged experts is very large, much greater than the different kinds of assessment data used in making judgments. This is because, for any particular technique, different schools of thought tend to develop with respect to the best way of coding and interpreting the sample of behavior used as a basis for judgments.

A person may acquire the reputation of being an "expert judge" by any of several routes. The most frequent route is to study with or be tutored by a person who already has such a reputation. If and when the protégé learns to make judgments with which the expert agrees, he is regarded as qualified to make such judgments "on his own." Even without special training he may achieve a reputation as an expert by working in a setting that permits his judgments to be reviewed by other professional persons. If, in their opinion, his judgments, based on his preferred techniques, tend to appear as generally correct, his reputation will grow. Note that in both cases the criterion of correctness of validity is a consensual one; in the first, the "master" concurs; in the second, one's immediate colleagues concur. Finally, one may become an expert "by proclamation" and by the judicious use of selected dramatic instances of correct assessment or predictions. Expertness as a judge is almost always a function of reputation; rarely is it a matter of demonstrated validity of the judgments made by the "expert."

PEER JUDGES

In view of the known fallibility of the ratings of one judge (even expert ones!) and the fact that the average ratings of many judges tend to be much more dependable, psychologists have increasingly utilized, especially in research settings, every member of a living or working group as judge of all others in the group. For example, every member of a fraternity can be asked to judge each of his brothers. While a group situation is a necessary condition for the collection of sociometric ratings, one's peers from different groups may be asked to provide ratings on any of the several kinds of rating scales.

A necessary condition for obtaining good ratings from peer judges is that members of the group have lived, worked and/or played with each other over a sufficiently long period so that everyone has had an opportunity to observe his fellow members in a variety of situations. Furthermore, the group used must be small enough so each member has been able to get to know all of his fellow members fairly well. Groups which meet these requirements and which have been effectively used in personality research include living groups such as fraternities, sororities, a section of a dormitory, squads or platoons in military organizations, work crews, etc. Although all members of any group are not likely to be equally good judges, the average rating of several peer judges has been found to provide remarkably useful assessments of many personality traits. In fact, for many personality variables, the average of several peer ratings constitute the best currently available measures, and, as such, are frequently used as criterion measures against which the scores of newly developed assessment devices are validated. The chief limitation of peer ratings grows out of the fact that they are available only (1) for those subjects who are members of a group which meets the requirements noted above, and (2) if it is possible to persuade all or most of the group's members to serve as judges. These requirements can usually be met in research settings—especially if the group members are paid to participate—but it is often difficult to obtain peer ratings in practical assessment situations.

Another situation in which it is possible to obtain and average the ratings of the same person by many judges is so rarely used that it has not yet been given a special name. The subject is rated not by professionals, not by his supervisor, not by his peers, but by persons below him in an organizational hierarchy. The first use of subordinates as judges appears to have occurred in 1927 with the development of the Purdue Rating Scale for Instructors (Remmers & Elliot, 1927–1960). Many teachers now routinely ask their students to rate both them and their course. A considerable body of evidence indicates that the average of such ratings by 20 or more students is highly stable from class to class and has sufficient validity to be of real value to any teacher who wishes to improve his teaching. Of course, there is no technical reason why similar ratings could not be obtained from subordinates for persons in other supraordinate positions: supervisors, managers, ministers, and even officers in the military services!

SELF-RATINGS

In addition to judging his associates, every human being is in the unique position of being able to serve as a judge or rater of himself. In fact, no other person has had such extended opportunity to observe one in such a wide variety of situations! In addition to the unusually rich collection of behavior samples, each person has the additional advantage of having "experienced" most of the observed behavior "from the inside" and has memories of these experiences as well as of the more objective aspects of his behavior in many settings.

It is not surprising then that psychologists have made extensive use of self-ratings, especially in personality research. Any of the several kinds of rating scales (except sociometric) may be used in collecting self-ratings. Although perhaps more subject to the several varieties of rating errors than are the ratings of others, self-ratings have been shown to be fairly consistent over time, especially if obtained under conditions which reduce the tendency "to see oneself through rose-colored glasses." For many traits, self-ratings have been found to be as valid, to correlate as highly, with peer ratings as the best available alternative measures of the same traits.

Of special interest is the fact that a person may be asked to rate not one but several possibly different "selves" depending on the nature of the instructional set, for example:

Social Self: "Rate yourself as you think others see you."
Real Self: "Rate yourself as you really think you are."
Ideal Self: "Rate yourself as you would ideally like to be."

While each of the resulting sets of ratings is of considerable intrinsic interest, many psychologists have been even more interested in the discrepancies of self-ratings obtained with different instructional sets, since these discrepancies may serve as useful assessments of other characteristics which the subject is not able to perceive or to rate directly. Thus considerable use has been made of the discrepancy between the "real self" and "ideal self" as a possible index of maladjustment. By obtaining successive self-ratings of both kinds at different stages of psychotherapy, one can ascertain whether or not the real-ideal discrepancy is being reduced—and, if so, whether as the result of changes in the perceived real self, the perceived ideal self, or both.

WHAT ARE THE CHARACTERISTICS OF GOOD JUDGES?

Because of the extensive use of persons as assessment instruments in a wide range of situations both in practice and research, many investigators have attempted to identify the salient characteristics of the "good judge." Since human beings show such marked individual differences on all other traits, it seems only reasonable to suppose that they differ widely in the ability to judge or rate their associates. The general acceptance of this belief is reflected in descriptive statements such as "He is a shrewd judge of people."

In order to determine the characteristics of good as contrasted with poor judges, it is first necessary to assess the ability of judges to judge others. A variety of ingenious procedures to measure this ability have been devised; an obvious one involves determining the accuracy with which judges can estimate or rate variables for which there are alternative highly reliable measures of accepted validity, such as height, weight, and I Q. In the absence of such alternative standard measures, it is common to determine the agreement (correlation) between the ratings of a single judge and the average ratings of several other judges. One may also ascertain how accurately a judge can predict the self-description of subjects, using a rating scale, an adjective checklist, or a set of Q-sort cards. Finally, it is possible to determine how well judges can predict future performance such as school grades, success on parole, progress in therapy, or amount of a product sold.

Methodologically, the problem of assessing the ability to judge is a very complex one because of a variety of contaminating variables such as the similarity of the judge and the ratee, and whether or not the judge likes or dislikes the persons being judged. Because of these and other even more involved considerations, our knowledge of the characteristics essential for a good judge is far from adequate. The problem is even more complicated by the fact that much evidence raises serious doubt as to whether there is a general trait of "ability to judge others." Instead, it appears that some persons are better at judging certain traits than others, or certain kinds of persons (children, delinquents, managerial personnel) than others. Furthermore, some persons seem to be able to utilize one kind of behavior sample more effectively than others in arriving at accurate judgments. In spite of these variations from judge to judge, present evidence tends to support a few broad generalizations.

AGE

Although elementary school children have been found to be capable of fairly dependable and useful ratings of some traits, there appears to be a continuing growth in the ability to judge others until the age of 30 or 40.

SEX

In spite of the popular belief in the superiority of women's intuition, there does not appear to be any real sex difference in the ability to judge others.

INTELLIGENCE

Although all studies concur in the finding that the good judge of others is more intelligent than the poor judge, this is hardly a surprising finding since the variables being rated are frequently rather abstract ones, requiring as a minimum an understanding of trait names and the ability to make logical inferences from behavior to trait ratings. However, the ability to judge others apparently involves more than general intelligence, since its correlations with tested intelligence are low, typically between .30 and .40.

SPECIAL TRAINING

As has been noted earlier, it is possible to improve both the reliability and validity of ratings by appropriate training of judges with respect to trait definitions, in the most effective use of a rating scale and in avoiding certain common types of rating errors. Furthermore, since ability to judge is associated with increasing age and intelligence, it is not surprising that most studies have shown college students to be better judges of others than are high school students. However, there appears to be some question as to whether professional training in clinical psychology, psychiatry, or social work enhances the ability to make better judgments or ratings. In fact, in the only study comparing the quality of judgments by persons with different kinds of graduate or professional training, Taft (1950) found that graduate students trained in experimental psychology did better than clinical psychologists and psychiatrists, and that graduate students in the physical sciences did better than either! Since in this study the ability to judge was assessed by comparing the ratings of each judge with the pooled ratings of all judges, it is of course possible that the ratings of the clinically trained and oriented judges were actually more nearly "true" ones than the pooled ratings of all judges.

An alternative and less charitable hypothesis for this unexpected finding is that persons who choose clinical specialization may do so in part because of their own emotional problems and hence are not able to be as objective in their appraisals of others as are persons less emotionally involved in working with people. There is also the possibility that the more elaborate personality theories embraced by clinicians are either not sound or that they lead judges to rely too heavily on nonrelevant behavioral cues in making inferences to traits. The deleterious effect of a wrong hypothesis is illustrated in Chapter VI, page 78.

Other investigators have found that the good judge tends to be superior in artistic or aesthetic sensitivity, that he is popular with others, but not highly sociable; that he himself is perceived by others as a complex—not easy-to-judge—person.

Guilford (1959) has succinctly summarized the available evidence regarding the characteristics associated with accuracy in rating oneself:

"The good self judge is highly intelligent, emotionally adjusted, and sociable. The good adjustment gives him freedom to become aware of his own weaknesses; and the sociability gives him the views that many others have of him. The good self judge is also said to have a good sense of humor and not to be conceited."

SUMMARY

For thousands of years man had to rely almost entirely on human judgment—his own and that of his fellows—for assessing the degree, amount, or extent of those characteristics of his world which he had perceived as real and important. Within the last hundred years, he has succeeded in developing techniques, methods, and instruments which have enabled him to measure most aspects of his physical world with great precision. In doing so, he was able for the first time to resolve many earlier debated issues regarding the independence of or relationships among physical attributes, dimensions, forces, etc.

In biology and the behavioral sciences, the development of acceptable and precise methods of measurement has been much slower. While these fields have profited from their ability to use the precise instruments of physical science, there are many important physiological, psychological, and social variables for which similarly precise and valid measuring instruments are not yet available. Just as the early physicists, chemists, and engineers had to rely heavily on the discriminations and ratings of human judges, behavioral scientists are still faced with the necessity of using them in the assessment of most of their variables. Although known to be far from a perfect measuring instrument, the human judge is indispensable in the assessment of most psychological characteristics. However, it is essential that we utilize these extremely crude measurements with full awareness of their limitations and in ways which permit their most effective use.

Our earlier discussion of reliability and validity dealt largely with measures or scores arrived at by the uniform scoring of responses made by subjects confronted with relatively standardized test situations. Standardized and objectively scored tests are now extensively used in the assessment of a wide variety of traits, but such tests are neither as popular nor as trusted as techniques that rely on human judgments and professional skills; such skills are often regarded as the most essential component of assessment techniques.

THE ISSUE

Which of these two markedly contrasting methods yields the better assessments? There is probably no issue on which practitioners are more sharply divided. One group takes the position that only by permitting the human assessor (1) to adapt the assessment situation to each subject, and (2) to serve both as a sensitive observer and as an interpreter of each subject's behavior can one hope to evaluate the really important aspects of a complex human personality and to predict future behavior. At the opposite extreme, another group argues that although human judges are still necessary in a wide variety of assessment situations and although the human mind is absolutely essential in the creation and development of new assessment techniques, nevertheless, the greater the involvement of human beings in the assessment process itself, the less is the reliability and validity of the resulting assessments. This debate is often referred to as the clinical vs. the statistical approach to assessment. Unfortunately, the label "clinical vs. statistical" is not truly descriptive of several intertwined issues. In many ways, "personal vs. impersonal" is more appropriate and is therefore used as the title of this chapter. However, no single pair of antonyms can possibly convey the degree of contrast between these two very different approaches to assessment. Proponents of each tend to use honorific adjectives to describe the approach they prefer and pejorative ones to designate the other approach. A reasonably balanced sample of these adjectives is shown in Table 1. As will be noted, many of these adjectives are value laden, so much so, in fact, as to suggest that the differences of the two groups are based more on beliefs than on empirical evidence. Regretably, this is all too true.

Table 1

Samples of evaluative adjectives used to describe the clinical and statistical approaches to assessment (after Meehl, 1954).

	That the clinical method is:	That the statistical method is:
Clinicians say:	dynamic, global, meaningful, holistic, subtle, sympathetic, configural, patterned, organized, rich, deep, genuine, sensitive, real, sophisticated, living, concrete, natural, true to life, understanding	mechanical, atomistic, additive, cut and dried, artificial, arbitrary, unreal, incomplete, dead, pedantic, fractionated, trivial, forced, static, superficial, rigid, sterile, academic, oversimplified, pseudoscientific, blind
Statisticians say:	mystical, transcendent, metaphysical, supermundane, vague, hazy, subjective, unscientific, unreliable, crude, private, unverifiable, qualitative, primitive, prescientific, sloppy, uncontrolled, careless, verbalistic, intuitive, muddleheaded	operational, communicable, verifiable, public, objective, reliable, behavioral, testable, rigorous, scientific, precise, careful, trustworthy, experimental, quantitative, down to earth, hardheaded, empirical, mathematical, sound

Persons committed to the personal approach insist on the freedom of a professionally trained individual to use his best judgment at any of several points or stages in the assessment process:

1. In the choice of behavior sample(s) to be used as a basis for assessment for each subject.

2. In the collection of assessment data; e.g., in the conduct of an interview; in the choice of and administration of tests, or in varying the nature of instructions to the subject.

3. In regard to the form in which the assessment data are recorded; this may range all the way from no record (i.e., reliance on memory), through brief or full notes, to complete sound recordings or even sound movies.

4. In the schema used for categorizing and tallying the categories of behavior observed and recorded.

5. In the weights assigned to observations or categories of behavior in making inferences regarding personality characteristics. This includes the freedom to weight or interpret the same response differently from subject to subject.

6. In regard to the format in which the assessment is reported. Clinicians prefer to prepare their reports in the form of an analytical "verbal portrait" of the person with an emphasis on description and the interpretation of his internal dynamics. Only rarely is the report in a form which permits any direct comparison of the subject with any other subject or any group of subjects. And even more rarely does the report include specific predictions regarding the future performance of the individual.

By contrast, the objectively oriented assessment psychologist views each of these freedoms to use professional judgment as a potential source of errors of assessment. He, therefore, insists on:

1. Using comparable behavior samples for all subjects for whom comparable assessments are to be made.

2. Standardized tests and uniform instructions.

3. The recording of all assessment data in a uniform and highly communicable fashion. If the data include ratings by human judges, these, too, must be collected in a uniform manner.

4. Objective and uniform procedures for categorizing and/or scoring the assessment data.

5. The use of uniform weights from subject to subject in making inferences from data to traits or from traits to future performance.

6. A uniform procedure for reporting the results of assessment, typically in the form of a profile of scores which facilitates direct comparison of one subject with another or with a known normative reference group, e.g., all applicants. Typically, a report will include specific predictions regarding the future behavior or performance of each subject.

Now, both of these extreme positions involve a series of reasonable and testable hypotheses. Exactly the same procedures which are used to evaluate the reliability and validity of test scores can be used in evaluating ratings, impressions, the decisions and predictions of clinicians, *providing that such assessments are systematically recorded and analyzed.* It should be noted that the extreme positions described above do not in any sense represent all possible positions. Relatively few clinicians, for example, would demand the freedom to use their best judgment at all stages of assessment. In fact, some are most insistent on the use of certain uniform procedures for data collection and codification. Similarly, the most objective of assessment psychologists often finds it necessary to use the fallible ratings of human judges, but such ratings are treated exactly as scores derived from objective tests in determining their contribution to the prediction of future behavior. Furthermore, it seems reasonable to suppose that either personal or impersonal methods might be superior for different aspects of assessment, for example, in the collection of assessment data, in making inferences from the data to personality variables, or in the prediction of future behavior. Conceivably, too, some combination of the two methods might prove to be better than either alone. For example, clinical observations might be used as the basis of trait ratings which are then fed into a computer; or a profile based on highly objective test scores might be used as a basis for clinical inferences.

Figure 1 represents an effort to summarize the major elements of both approaches to assessment. It is not possible, on a two-dimensional diagram, to include all of the many elements of the process or to emphasize several possible variants of them. For example, standardized tests may be administered by one person and objectively scored by the same person or by a different person or by an electronic test scoring machine. By contrast, one person typically administers a projective test, records and codes the responses of the subject, and then makes inferences about the subject's trait structure. Similarly, the person who conducts an interview is usually the same person who makes inferences about the subject on the basis of the subject's performance in the interview. Note that these are the usual conditions but are not necessary conditions. If a subject's responses are appropriately and fully recorded, the process of using them to make inferences about his trait structure may equally well be carried out by a different person or by several different persons, thus making it possible to determine the amount of interjudge agreement. If two or more clinicians use the same assessment behavior to make independent predictions regarding the future behavior of subjects, it becomes possible to compare their "predictive validity."

Not shown in Figure 1 are other possibilities, referred to above, such as using clinical ratings of traits for statistical prediction. Also, a

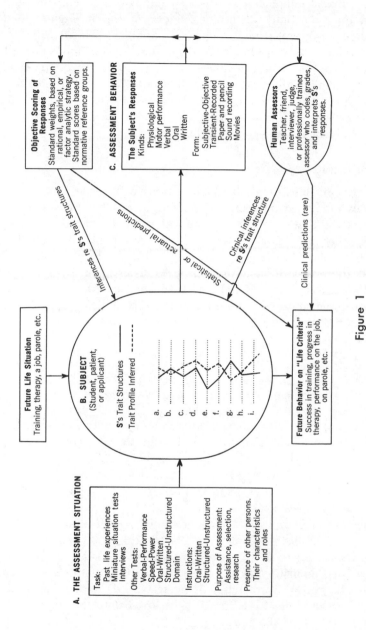

Figure 1

Schematic diagram showing the major elements in the assessment process.

human assessor could use objectively derived trait profiles as a partial basis for clinical inferences. It was also impossible to emphasize in the diagram the potentially disturbing effects on the inferences made of many often uncontrolled methodological variables such as: (1) the relative social desirability of alternative responses, (2) the subject's tendency to answer "yes" or "true" (acquiescence), (3) the use of the same responses to make inferences about different traits (multiple keying), (4) the several kinds of rating errors discussed in Chapter 6, and (5) the use of incorrect weights in scoring, or (6) the use of theories in interpreting the subject's assessment behavior.

THE EVIDENCE

In view of the strongly held convictions with respect to the relative superiority of the personal and impersonal approaches to assessment and because of the tremendous social importance of the millions of decisions about people made daily on the basis of assessments, it might be supposed that definitive evidence had been obtained to judge the relative merits of these very different approaches to assessment. Regretfully, such is not the case. In 1954, Meehl reviewed all available studies that provided a comparison of the validities of these contrasting approaches and concluded that there are:

". . . depending upon one's standards for admission as relevant, from 16 to 20 studies involving a comparison of clinical and actuarial methods, in all but one of which the predictions made actuarially were either approximately equal or superior to those made by a clinician."

As may be imagined, this conclusion was viewed with much dismay and even skepticism by clinicians who contended that the comparisons made by Meehl did not do justice to clinical methods.

More recently, Sawyer (1966) systematically reviewed the evidence of 45 available studies; this evidence permitted 75 comparisons of clinical and nonclinical methods of assessment. In his analysis, Sawyer categorized each set of findings in a manner which permitted a comparison of the relative validities resulting from the clinical versus the "mechanical," or statistical, methods of (1) *data combination*, (2) *data collection*, and (3) various combinations or syntheses of the two methods, e.g., clinical trait ratings statistically combined, or statistical predictions used as a partial basis for clinical prediction. With respect to the method of data combination, Sawyer concludes,

"Like Meehl's review, the present analysis finds the mechanical mode of combination always equal to or superior to the clinical mode; moreover, this is true whether the data were collected clinically or mechanically. Clinical combination actually predicts less well with data collected by both modes than with only mechanically collected data, and clinical combination that includes a mechanical prediction is inferior to the mechanical composite alone."

Although Sawyer's summary of the evidence provides little support for those committed to the clinical approach to assessment, the evidence from a few studies suggests that the most accurate predictions of future behavior are those based on a mechanical-statistical combination of both clinically and mechanically collected data. In Sawyer's words, "This suggests that the clinician may be able to contribute most not by direct prediction but by providing, in objective form, judgments to be combined mechanically." He is, of course, referring to the use of ratings by human judges which provide crude but useful measures of traits not presently assessable by objective techniques.

IMPACT ON ASSESSMENT PRACTICES

Strange as it may seem, the accumulation of evidence such as just cited has had almost no perceptible impact on assessment practices. The most extensively used and the most confidently used assessment procedures are still those which depend very heavily on the human being as an integral and often the major component of the technique! These are of three general kinds:

1. Teacher-made and graded essay tests and examinations. Literally millions of such tests are constructed and graded annually in spite of the fact that repeated studies indicate relatively low reliability and validity of the grades based on them. If graded by the same teacher on two separate occasions, the resulting grades are likely to vary considerably; if independently graded by two different readers, there is even less agreement between the two sets of marks; the lowest correlations are found when students are assessed on the same subject matter with two different sets of essay questions written and graded by different teachers. However, these correlations, though low, tend to be positive, so that course grades based on several tests tend to be more reliable and valid than the mark on any single test. Finally, grade-point averages based on the grades of many courses tend to have reasonably respectable levels of reliability and validity.

2. Interviews such as those used in personnel selection. This is by all odds the most widely used assessment technique in industry and is becoming increasingly popular in spite of repeated demonstrations of relatively low interjudge reliability and predictive validity of assessments by interviewers (Ulrich and Trumbo, 1965).

3. Projective techniques such as the Rorschach, TAT, or Draw-A-Person Tests. It has been estimated that at least a million Rorschachs are administered, scored, and interpreted each year at a cost of some five

million professional man hours. Yet the evidence for the validity of such costly assessments, even by presumed experts, is very discouraging.

In considering reasons for the typically low reliabilities and validities repeatedly reported for assessments based on these three classes of techniques, it should be noted that all three share certain common characteristics:

1. The assessment situation is characterized by (1) relatively few questions, items, cards, or problems, and/or (2) relatively little structure, i.e., the instructions are such as to permit or even encourage widely different responses by different subjects.

2. The assessment itself usually depends primarily on the judgment of a single individual in making the inferential leap from observed behaviors to assessment. The teacher, the interviewer, or the projective expert serves as the "scoring key" and weights each of the observed pieces of assessment data to arrive at his final assessment, be it a grade, a rating, a decision to accept or not accept an applicant, or the diagnosis of a patient.

If the same person functions as the test constructor, test administrator, and "scoring key," the reliability and the validity of the resulting assessments must be evaluated for each user of the technique. The resulting values may or may not be typical of those of another person using the same technique. It is widely believed that some persons are far more skillful than others in utilizing these techniques which rely so heavily on the skills and judgment of a single individual. While the hypothesis of varying degrees of expertise seems a reasonable one, there is very little evidence either to support or reject it. This is the case because it is rare that different judges assess the same individuals and thus provide the data necessary to compute interjudge agreement or to determine the relative validities of their independent judgments. In many instances, it has proven difficult to persuade professionals who use these techniques to record their assessments in a form that would permit the statistical analysis necessary for estimating either reliabilities or validities. This is true in spite of the fact that clinicians need not record assessments in numerical form, since appropriate statistical techniques are available for computing correlations between categorical variables such as pass-fail, accept-reject, normal, neurotic, or psychotic, etc.

CONDITIONS WHICH LOWER THE RELIABILITIES OF PERSONAL ASSESSMENTS

On the basis of available evidence, it seems likely that the low reliability of techniques relying heavily on the human element is primarily the result of the relatively small and/or the relatively nonuniform samples of behavior elicited by the assessment situation. Every student has experienced the anxiety that results from knowing that a final examination is likely to ask about but five of perhaps a hundred topics covered in a course. The standard Rorschach test consists of only 10 stimulus cards; and Rorschach experts insist that each card is so unique in the responses which it elicits that it is not appropriate to estimate the reliability of scores by computing separate scores based on the odd- and even-numbered cards.[1] While an essay examination, an interview, or a Rorschach test usually involves behavior extending over an hour or more, the lack of structure in the test situation typically results in a marked lack of comparability of much of the behavior elicited from subject to subject.

A second probable basis for the low reliability of measures derived from this group of assessment techniques is that different users do not score, evaluate, or interpret the obtained behavioral samples in a uniform manner. If the same set of behavior is observed and rated by two or more judges or if the same recorded protocol is coded or rated by independent judges, the amount of interjudge agreement may be determined. Note, though, that any such index of interjudge agreement does not constitute any of the three kinds of reliability discussed in Chapter 4. It is entirely possible to train judges to agree closely in their coding or scoring of assessment data even though the sample of data is not adequate for inferring a person's true position on any trait continuum. Lack of interjudge agreement in scoring, however, inevitably points to the lack of reliability of the scores (or ratings) of one or both of the judges.

CONDITIONS WHICH REDUCE VALIDITIES OF PERSONAL ASSESSMENTS

Since, as was noted in Chapter 4, the reliability of any set of measures places an upper limit on their validity for any purpose, the primary basis for the low reported validities of measures derived from highly personal techniques is unquestionably a function of their low reliability. Another reason for their low validity is that persons using these techniques, especially interviews and projective techniques, rely very heavily on the rational strategies for making inferences from assessment data to psychological meaning. To the extent that one's hypotheses and speculations are not correct, inferences based on them are bound to be lacking in validity. Even when assessment psychologists committed to a heavy reliance on the human component of a technique are willing to provide assessments amenable to statistical analysis, we are still confronted with the difficult and sometimes insoluble problem of ascertain-

[1]Curiously, however, they approve of adding similarly coded responses from the different cards!

ing the manner in which the assessor (judge, interviewer, etc.) weights different bits of data in arriving at his rating or decision. Only rarely are data available to permit an analysis of this kind.

In one such instance, the author was able to identify the source of the low validity of a specific set of ratings. In a study of the usefulness of a series of 100 variables for predicting the performance of medical students (Kelly, 1957), it was found that the best single predictor variable was the student's overall grade point ratio in his premedical college program. In the medical school involved, all applicants were also interviewed by one of the five members of a committee on admissions. After the interview, all five members of the committee met to review the student's total academic record and test scores, read his references, and hear the evaluation of the committee member who had interviewed him; each then made an independent rating predicting his performance in medical school. In spite of the fact that all members of the committee had access to this extensive body of information for each applicant, no member of the committee produced a set of ratings which predicted a student's academic performance in medical school as well as a single variable, his overall "premed" grade point average. In arriving at his ratings, each of the committee members was free to assign a weight to each of the pieces of information available to him as he felt appropriate. A detailed analysis of the interrelationships among these potential predictor variables and the relationship of each to subsequently earned grades in medical school revealed at least one source of the rather low validity of the ratings of the judges. In arriving at their ratings, four of the five judges had tended (unknowingly) to give a plus weight to "number of credit hours in biology" whereas this variable was in fact negatively correlated with both the premedical grade average and with later grades in medical school. Apparently, students with poorer overall grade records felt that it would improve their chances of being admitted to medical school if they demonstrated their motivation to study medicine by taking additional nonrequired courses in biology. In this instance, at least, it seems that the applicants were reasonably astute in predicting the rating behavior of the members of the committee on admissions!

REASONS FOR THE WIDESPREAD POPULARITY OF PERSONALIZED ASSESSMENT TECHNIQUES

It is paradoxical, indeed, that those assessment procedures which are most valued and most widely used in educational institutions, in industry, and in psychiatric clinics and hospitals are those which, on the basis of available evidence, typically yield assessments low in both reliability and validity. Even more striking is the fact that assessment practice is so little affected by the steady accumulation of evidence pointing to low reliabilities or validities of such assessments. Why should this situation exist? It is evident that the persons who are responsible for the choice among alternative assessment techniques and their continued use in practice are using criteria other than those of reliability and validity. Let us consider several possible alternate bases for the choice of the more personalized techniques of assessment.

First of all, in the work-a-day world, the professional or occupational roles of some people demand that they make decisions about individuals, decisions which are of great importance, not only to the individual but to an organization or to society at large. Thus, teachers must evaluate the performance of their students and report some kind of a mark or grade; selection interviewers are asked to make a yes-no decision to accept or reject each applicant interviewed. In the case of possible mental illness, someone must decide whether or not a patient is sufficiently disturbed to require hospitalization, even though it may be involuntary. In all of these examples, the decision concerns an individual person, and the assessor is poignantly aware of the potential harm that would result from an incorrect assessment and decision. It is hardly surprising that he seeks for and eventually selects assessment procedures which provide him, the assessor, with a feeling of confidence in his assessments and/or decisions. For him to use tests known to yield fallible scores would inevitably increase his own anxiety on the job.

Now, in the first place, it is a painful fact that we do not yet have techniques which yield measures with demonstrably high reliabilities and validities for most of the psychological variables that must be assessed in the situations mentioned above. Even the best of our assessment procedures yield scores with known errors of measurement and unsatisfactorily low validities. Furthermore, the factual evidence regarding their fallibility is publicly available in test manuals and in the Mental Measurements Yearbooks (Buros, ed., 1965). Confronted with this unpleasant state of affairs, it is easy to understand how assessors "on the firing line" are tempted to use techniques which they believe yield more accurate and valid assessments rather than techniques with only modest levels of demonstrated reliability and validity.

Secondly, whenever a human being constitutes the major component of an assessment technique, he is in the pleasant position of being able to believe that a technique *as used by him* yields assessments which are more nearly correct than he could obtain with a less personalized technique. Because he personally observes a subject, tailors the assessment situation to the subject, and varies the weights assigned to each piece of assessment data, the assessor fancies that he can arrive at a more nearly correct assessment than if he uses standardized techniques with uniform scoring weights for all subjects. And, even though he may be aware of the considerable body of evidence regarding the low reliability and validity of assessment techniques that permit or encourage variations from standardized procedures, he can always believe that, because of his more extensive experience and greater expertise, *his* assessments are both reliable and valid. Since it is rare for the assessor to collect data in the form necessary to determine the actual validity or reliability of his own assessments, he finds it easy to continue to believe in their infallibility.

A third possible reason for the widely held belief in the superiority of assessment techniques relying heavily on the human component is that many of these techniques do in fact yield considerable information about each subject. A one-hour selection interview, for example, certainly permits the interviewer to learn many facts concerning an applicant. Intuitively, it would seem that the more information one has available, the better or wiser the decision will be regarding the applicant. Furthermore, a wide array of information plus "having seen the person" results in a feeling on the part of the interviewer that he "knows" or "understands" the subject and is, therefore, capable of making wise decisions concerning him.

However, as we have noted, the collection of information constitutes but the first step of the assessment process. Life history data, whether collected by an interview, an autobiography, or by a structured biographical inventory, must be processed in some manner (categorized, weighted, scored, etc.) in order to arrive at inferences regarding the characteristics of a person or his future behavior. And while all information about a person is potentially useful assessment data, all pieces of information are not equally relevant in making different kinds of inferences about him. Inferences are valid only to the degree (1) that they are based on *relevant* data and (2) that the relevant data are optimally weighted (with respect to both sign and magnitude) for the inference made. To the extent that inferences are based even in part on nonrelevant information, their validity is inevitably impaired. Although it may seem contrary to common sense, it is also possible that the availability of too much information may tempt the human asssessor to use some non-relevant data in making invalid inferences about a subject. This possibility becomes a probability when, as is typically the case, the assessor relies primarily on a rational strategy for making inferential leaps.

An alternate possibility is that, in spite of the availability of a wide array of information, the human assessor may choose to use only limited portions of it in arriving at his inference or decision. An extreme example of this possibility is dramatically illustrated by the following experience. During World War II, the author had two conversations with a Naval Reserve officer assigned to a Naval Aviation Cadet Selection Board. At the time of the first conversation, early in the war, this inexperienced nonpilot interviewer pleaded for advice as to how to identify promising vs. unpromising flight cadets in a selection interview. Several months later, the same officer, having interviewed hundreds of applicants, announced confidently that he had discovered one question which enabled him to eliminate the poor risks. The question was,

"Have you ever collected stamps?"

His rationale was simple: "Anyone who has collected stamps is an introvert, and introverts do not make good Naval aviators." It is of interest that he had developed his miniature theory and his assessment procedure without any feedback regarding the success or failure in flight training of the young men whom he had already recommended! Regardless of the actual validity of either his theory or his methods of assessment, he had found a procedure which eliminated his earlier anxiety regarding the correctness of the vital day-to-day decisions which he was forced to make.

SPURIOUS CRITERIA OF VALIDITY

The high esteem with which they are held and the continued widespread use of techniques relying heavily on the human assessor suggests that decisions regarding their use are based on considerations other than demonstrated evidence of their validity. Stated another way, their proponents appear to be using one or more of several spurious criteria of validity. Although these are not completely independent, it is useful to define four varieties:

"FACE VALIDITY"

Using this criterion, a test or technique is judged to measure "so and so" simply because it looks like it should. In other words, it seems reasonable to suppose that the behavior sampled and the manner in which responses are interpreted should lead to valid inferences regarding the trait that is purportedly being assessed. In assessing educational achievement, experts can agree reasonably well as to whether a given sample of test questions constitutes an appropriate basis for valid inferences regarding achievement in a specified field of study. In fact, the consensual validity utilized in the construction of educational achievement tests represents nothing more than generally agreed upon face validity. In the other trait domains, it is almost impossible to secure consensus among presumed experts as to what a test is really measuring, yet the value of many assessment procedures is judged by some users almost entirely on this basis. There is no objection to a test having face validity—in fact, it is desirable—but appearance alone is not enough!

"VALIDITY BY FIAT"

If the producer of an assessment device is in a position of authority *vis-à-vis* persons being assessed, he may simply declare that his technique or test measures "so and so." As an extreme example, a teacher of Subject X may use any type or combination of behavior samples he chooses in assessing the achievement of students in his class. Even if he chooses to base his course grades primarily on class attendance, the grades would be treated in the school records as measures of achievement in Subject X. His students might complain, but his grades would be valid by fiat!

Validity by fiat may also occur as the result of someone's high status—as when a prominent person develops a new assessment technique purported to yield a measure of creativity, rigidity, or some other personality trait. If the creator of the technique has a reputation as being highly competent and responsible, many persons will be willing to begin using his technique and to believe in the validity of inferences based on it simply because it was developed by Prof. A. or Dr. B., who proclaimed the technique valid. The likelihood of acceptance of validity by fiat is enhanced if the developer of the technique defends its inferences on the basis of a theory of personality already embraced by the potential users of the technique.

"EXPERIENCED VALIDITY"

Many devotees defend the use of assessment techniques with little or no demonstrated validity solely on the grounds that its use provides them, the users, with an "understanding of the subject," whether the subject is a student, applicant, client, or patient. Note that this criterion is entirely internal to the assessor; the technique is judged to be valid to the extent that it provides the user with a subjective sense of the correctness of the inferences that he makes with it. Some users go so far as to insist that this is the only appropriate criterion of validity—that it is "not fair" to ask for evidence of either construct or practical validity of the assessments they make.

While there is no reason to deny to the user of any assessment technique the personal satisfaction of such perceived or experienced validity, these reported "experiences of truth" are more akin to the aesthetic appreciation of works of art than to scientific evidence. That "experienced understanding" does not constitute an adequate criterion for the actual validity of the resulting description and interpretation of personality is most clearly evidenced by the fact that two assessors, using different techniques, may each arrive at a personally satisfying "understanding" of the same subject, yet a comparison of the two independent formulations of the subject's personality shows almost no correspondence. Obviously some external criterion is needed to determine which of the two "understandings" of the same subject is the more valid one.

"FAITH VALIDITY"

As suggested by the label, faith validity refers to a belief, usually strongly held on the part of the user, *that a technique as used by him* yields accurate and correct information and thus permits making valid inferences and good decisions about another human being. One may begin using a technique with but little initial faith; but after using it over a period of time and having perceived the essential correctness of the decisions one has made on the basis of it, one is likely to develop increasing confidence both in the technique and in one's own expertise in its use.

Why should these spurious criteria of validity be so widely used as basis for the choice and continued use of certain assessment techniques in actual practice? The author ventures three interlocking hypotheses. Such spurious criteria all serve:

1. To reduce anxiety on the part of the user of the technique regarding the correctness of the resulting assessments.
2. To enhance the self-esteem of the human assessor and the techniques they presume to justify.
3. To reduce any sense of need to check the actual validity of the assessments—or of oneself!

Strange as it may seem, professional persons committed to assessment techniques in which the human element is all important rarely venture to check the amount of agreement of two independent sets of personality descriptions—much less the accuracy of predictions of the future behavior of the persons they assess. It is easy to rationalize the failure to do so on the grounds that "staff time does not permit" or "no suitable criteria are available," but the author suggests that there is a far more basic reason for the failure to make systematic evaluations of the actual validities of assessments: As long as one does not do so, one can retain his "faith."

The hazards of checking on the congruence of independent assessments were dramatically illustrated by an experiment carried out by two clinical psychologists on the staff of a neuropsychiatric hospital.[2] Dr. A. regarded himself as expert in the use of the Rorschach technique and Dr. B. had much faith in the validity of his personality assessments based on Bender-Gestalt drawings. Each had high regard for the professional competence of the other, and both were completely convinced that their independent assessments of patients showed a high degree of agreement. Because of the strength of their convictions, they decided to

[2]This experiment was carried out many years ago. The results were never published but were communicated personally to the author by the two investigators.

carry out a piece of research to refute recently published research casting doubt on the agreement of independent personality assessments based on their two favorite techniques (Kelly and Fiske, 1951). They therefore planned a simple experiment: Each would use his preferred technique as a basis for assessing the next 50 newly admitted patients on 20 traits that they themselves had chosen and believed they could rate validly. They would then compute the correlations between their independent ratings for each of the 20 traits. (They had previously ranked the 20 traits on the basis of the degree of agreement which they expected to find in their ratings.)

The experiment was carried out as planned, but the investigators were scarcely prepared for what they found: The amount of agreement between their independently arrived at ratings was just about what would have been obtained had all of their trait ratings been assigned by some game of chance. For approximately half of the 20 traits, the correlations were positive, and for the other half, negative. Ironically, the highest *negative* correlation (−.40) was for the trait "Level of Anxiety" for which they had predicted the greatest agreement in their ratings!

In view of the strong convictions of these two clinicians that their independently arrived at assessments generally agreed, the same data were analyzed by computing an index of profile congruence of the two independently rated 20-trait profiles for individual patients. In general, the two independently rated profiles for the same patient were strikingly similar; however, the two profiles for the same patient were no more similar than Dr. A.'s profile for one patient and Dr. B.'s profile for another patient! What had happened was that both Dr. A. and Dr. B. had unknowingly tended to rate all patients in terms of a shared stereotype of the typical patient in that hospital. Tragically, this shared stereotype of the typical patient proved to be the only basis for the perceived agreement in their assessments of specific patients. It is difficult to believe that two professionally trained persons could allow themselves to be so badly deceived by such a simple artifact. However, a number of others who have investigated apparent interjudge agreement have found that, after eliminating the effect of common biases in ratings, there remains but very little similarity in independently rated profiles based on different assessment techniques (Goldberg and Werts, 1966; Malcolm, 1952).

While reliance on spurious criteria of validity may in part explain the extreme popularity of assessments that have repeatedly been shown to have low reliabilities and validities, there are still other reasons for their continued uncritical acceptance and use by institutions and organizations and by the public in general.

1. Certain techniques, especially essay examinations and interviews,

were used long before methods were developed for evaluating either reliability or validity. Long established and traditional practices tend to continue in spite of extensive evidence suggesting their great fallibility.

2. All of the techniques in question yield (or appear to yield) a broad range of information and can therefore be used for many different purposes. For example, an essay examination *can* be used as a basis for judging neatness, grammar, vocabulary, and ability to allocate one's time, as well as achievement in a course. An interview may be used to obtain information or to judge personal characteristics which an organization regards as important in its employees, even though they may not be related to job performance, e.g., race, religious affiliation, or leisure-time activities. The same interview may also serve to orient an applicant with respect to an organization or to sell him on the desirability of deciding to accept a position with the organization.

3. An institution or organization utilizing techniques of low validity is rarely inclined to question the validity of the assessment procedures which it has directed to be used—or the judgment of the professional staff it has employed and to which it has assigned responsibilities for assessment.

4. Whenever someone questions the usefulness of any particular assessment procedure, it is always possible to defend its value on the basis of selected dramatic case histories of "hits" or correct decisions and very easy to overlook the much more frequent "misses."

5. Finally, as Forer (1949) demonstrated, human beings—even college students—are sufficiently gullible so that it is a simple matter to prepare a personality description which will be judged as remarkably accurate by almost all subjects *even though it contains no unique information whatsoever!* The trick is to construct the sketch on the basis of a judicious combination of three kinds of statements:

1. Those which are true of all people, e.g., "At times, you have serious doubts as to whether you have made the right decision or done the right thing."
2. Those which are so flattering that each person is highly pleased to have them used about themselves, e.g., "You have a tendency to be critical of yourself."
3. Those which are so ambiguous that each person can interpret them in a manner which best fits him, e.g., "You have found it unwise to be too frank in revealing yourself to others."

IN CONCLUSION

The assessment of human characteristics has been going on for thousands of years, largely on the basis of the judgments of one person by another. Literally millions of inferences based on remarkably diverse samples of behavior are made every day and used as the basis of important decisions in the lives of individuals.

A very large proportion of all current human assessments is carried out by persons presumed, on the basis of their training and/or experience, to be relatively expert in making correct inferences with the use of a particular method, technique, or sample of behavior. During the last 50 years, psychologists, using newly developed statistical methods, have carried out hundreds of evaluations of assessment procedures. The results of these studies have been both shocking and sobering. Many formerly revered and confidently used techniques (phrenology, physiognomy, and graphology) were found to yield completely useless inferences. Assessments based on other widely accepted procedures (essay tests, selection interviews and projective tests) have been found to be far more fallible than anyone ever thought possible. Much research has been carried out in an effort to identify the sources of error in such assessments and to develop alternative techniques capable of providing more reliable and valid assessments. For the most part, these newer procedures tended to be more structured and more objective than more traditional techniques.

On the basis of what is now a substantial body of research findings, it must be concluded that the greater the role an individual human assessor is permitted to play to the total assessment process, that is, the more his individual judgment determines the behavior samples on which the assessment is based and the nature of the inferences made, the more the resulting assessments tend to be found lacking in both reliability and validity. And even in those instances in which a highly personalized technique has been found to yield useful assessments (e.g., some selection interviews), equally valid assessments of the same traits can usually be achieved by the use of relatively simple objective techniques (e.g., a personality inventory or life-history questionnaire) which are less costly in terms of professional time (Cronbach and Gleser, 1965).

All of this research evidence has had but minimal impact on the choice of assessment procedures used in practice. Possible explanations were suggested for the continued reliance on, and widespread acceptance of, assessment techniques relying heavily on the role of the human assessor in spite of mounting evidence of their relatively low reliability and validity.

We are forced to conclude that, as an instrument for the assessment of human characteristics, the human assessor is far less than adequate either for routine use in basic psychological research or in applied practice. Does it follow that there is no role for the psychologist in assessment? The answer is an emphatic "No!" The tasks ahead and the critical roles that must be played by human beings in the development of improved assessment methods are matters to which we turn in the final chapter.

Although human beings must serve initially as the only available instruments for identifying variables in any field of science, human judgments are so fallible that they do not constitute an adequate basis for the development of a science. Scientists in every field have found it necessary to develop techniques and methods that provide more objective measures of variables than are permitted by human judgments. Lord Kelvin, the famous British physicist, once observed, "Until you have measured it, you don't know what you are talking about." Likewise, the usefulness of knowledge in the solution of practical problems is closely related to the level of accuracy with which a science assesses its phenomena and variables.

PRESENT STATUS

The assessment of most human characteristics is still in a relatively primitive stage, but reliable and valid assessment is critical for the development of the science of psychology, and of great importance in the practical affairs of man. Only within the last half century have psychologists become fully aware of the very serious limitations of traditional methods of human assessment. Encouraging progress has occurred in the development of objective measures of a few traits, notably certain aptitudes and educational achievement. While thousands of new tests and techniques have been developed (and marketed) for the assessment of other traits, a relatively small proportion of them have been shown to yield measures sufficiently reliable and valid to be useful in applied settings. In the absence of really good tools for assessing important noncognitive variables, both traditional methods and newer methods relying heavily on expert but empirically unsupported judgment and inference tend to dominate the applied practice of assessment.

The relatively brief history of psychology as an empirical science has been characterized by a number of significant cross currents, each of which has had a definite impact on assessment. The early experimental psychologists were primarily concerned with discovery of general laws to describe the exact relationships between variables such as stimulus intensity and sensation, or the shape of the curves of learning and forgetting. In their search for general laws, they were looking for relationships that are true of all persons. To the extent that individual differences among subjects showed up in the results of an experiment, they were regarded as errors rather than phenomena of intrinsic interest. Even today, the most widely used statistical technique[1] for inferring that a true difference exists between groups of subjects tests the differences of means and overlooks the marked individual differences among the members of each group. By contrast, following the lead of Galton in England and James McKeen Cattell in the United States, another group of psychologists became intrigued with the range of variety of individual differences, the origins of such differences, and the relationship among these differences. Unfortunately, there was all too little communication between the two groups of psychologists. Each tended to develop its own theories, methods, and body of knowledge. The resulting schism was so great that Cronbach (1960), in a brilliant review of the situation, called his essay, "The Two Disciplines of Scientific Psychology."

Although each of these disparate groups of psychologists could point with pride to accomplishments and each could claim useful appplications of the new knowledge and/or methods which it had developed, their accomplishments were viewed as relatively hollow by a third group of psychologists who felt that both experimental psychologists and psychologists concerned with individual differences had failed to attack the most essential problem of psychology, that of understanding the behavior of the individual person. Historically, questions regarding the whys of human behavior had been treated by philosophers who sought to support their theories by logical analysis and illustrative examples rather than systematically collected empirical evidence. In fact, many of the early psychologists were primarily philosophers both by education and orientation. But to the extent that they were beginning to identify with psychology as an empirical science, such persons yearned for a better theory of human behavior—one more congruent with the deterministic orientation of the young science of psychology.

Almost as if in answer to this yearning, Sigmund Freud proposed his revolutionary theory of motivation, one which promised to explain all individual behavior, both normal and abnormal. Based on his astute observations of neurotic patients, Freud's encompassing theory proved to be an extremely challenging one which has had a tremendous impact on the present day psychological theories of personality. However, because the methods of psychoanalysis were primarily clinical, there was but little communication between those who embraced psychoanalytic theories and those committed to either of the other "two disciplines" of psychology. The result was that there tended to become "three

[1]Analysis of variance.

disciplines" of psychology, each guided by its own problems, theories, and methods.[2]

The situation is even more confused by the existence of traditional methods of assessment that are widely trusted. The result, as we have seen, is that there are presently many divergent methods of assessment, each regarded as superior by one group or another. No assessment procedures yield measures that are generally agreed upon as valid for measures of key personality variables. This has seriously impeded the development of a science of personality. There are many theories of personality and hundreds of posited variables, but remarkably little consensus among theorists regarding the definition of and/or the measurement of most personality variables.

EXPERIMENTAL PSYCHOLOGY

Experimental psychologists are still primarily concerned with process variables like motivation and learning, as contrasted with individual differences. While they are scrupulously careful to define operationally and to measure carefully the variables with which they deal, they are typically not interested in the behavior of individual subjects, but in the differences in the average behavior of subjects receiving different treatments. For this reason, they are generally not concerned with the reliability of the measures of individual subjects. For their purposes, it suffices to know that the mean of an experimental group is significantly different from that of a control group, thus justifying the conclusion that the treatment "makes a difference." Even when experimental psychologists use a personality variable, e.g., anxiety, as related to rate of eyelid conditioning (Taylor, 1951), they tend to use groups of S's selected to represent "high" and "low" anxiety levels rather than to analyze the correlations of anxiety and rate of conditioning on a subject-by-subject basis. And, for the most part, experimental psychologists have been singularly unconcerned with the construct validity of their measures. In fact, it is relatively rare that two or more alternative operational measures of the same process are obtained for the same subjects. Thus learning may be assessed by the number of trials to learn a maze, by rate of bar pressing, or by trials to learn pairs of associated words. Only in the last few years has critical attention been given to whether all of these are equally valid measures of "learning."

[2]A notable recent exception is the work of Gerald Blum who utilizes rigorous experimental and statistical methods in testing hypotheses based on psychoanalytic theory. See Blum's volume in this series: *Psychodynamics: The Science of Unconscious Mental Forces.*

PERSONALITY THEORY AND RESEARCH

Freud's original and challenging theory of psychoanalysis and his own modifications of it served as a stimulus for the development of many further developments in personality theory with the result that psychology is now confronted with far more hypothesized personality variables than it has been able to assess in a satisfactory manner. Psychologists oriented to the experimental testing of personality theories have for the most part followed the model of traditional experimental psychology, i.e., the classical two-variable experiment with the extremely modest goal of establishing a statistically significant difference or relationship. In so doing, they are not usually concerned with the reliability of their measures but only with establishing the fact that some average performance of a group high on Variable X differs from the average of a group low on Variable X. *For this purpose,* a relatively crude or unreliable measure may serve to demonstrate a true difference between the means of groups of subjects. For example, a five-word test of spelling ability with a reliability of only .20 is entirely adequate to compare the average spelling ability of 1,000 eighth grade students in City A with 1,000 students in City B. Such a test, however, because of its very low reliability, would be virtually useless in comparing the spelling ability of any two individual students. Unfortunately, this critical consideration is often overlooked by persons who rely on empirically demonstrated group differences to justify the use of the same method for the assessment of individuals.

The widespread use of the classical two-variable experiment by personality psychologists has also tended to slow up the development of new knowledge in the field of personality. Since all experience indicates that assessment techniques rarely yield pure measures of any variable, one can never be sure in a two-variable experiment which of the two (or more) components of a complex variable is involved in the differences or relationships found. Only by using more complex multivariate research designs involving alternative methods for assessing variables can one be reasonably confident regarding the proper interpretation of his results. However, experimental personality psychologists have been generally slow in utilizing such multivariate research designs.

THE STRUCTURAL ANALYSIS OF PERSONALITY

Just as personality theorists are confronted with too many hypothesized but unsubstantiated variables, those psychologists who have been less interested in theory and more interested in the measurement of traits find themselves with literally thousands of potential measures of human characteristics but with a tragic lack of systematic order among them. Thanks to factor analysis, some progress has been made toward establishing clusters of variables that correlate highly with each other but not with other clusters of variables. But there is still almost no agreement regarding the minimum number of dimensions needed to provide an adequate description of the human personality, whether these basic-reference dimensions are in fact independent or are correlated with each other, and what labels should be used to designate the most essential variables.

ASSESSMENT PRACTICE

The most characteristic thing about the practice of assessment is its diversity. As we have noted in Chapter 6, the most popular and trusted methods are those relying heavily on human judgment and inference. Certain of these (e.g., the selection interview) were developed long before the days of scientific psychology and have sufficient face validity for people to continue to use them uncritically in a wide range of practical situations even where more objective techniques are available. Other methods (projective techniques and diagnostic interviews) rely heavily on inferences based on unconfirmed hypotheses involving poorly defined variables. But because they lead to total assessments that have apparent validity for the assessor, these techniques are highly valued and extensively used, often with little concern for the actual validity of the assessments which they yield. Finally, present day assessments with the highest demonstrated reliability and validity are those developed on a purely empirical basis (e.g., weighted responses to a biographical inventory or multiple-regression equations using objective test scores). While of demonstrated utility in a wide range of applications, such highly impersonal methods tend to be rejected by users because they do not explain the "whys" of behavior. Furthermore, empirically derived weights tend to be highly specific to the situation for which they were developed and hence their application to another situation is hazardous (e.g., the best weights for predicting success as an insurance salesman may not have any validity for predicting the performance of used car salesmen).

TOWARD BETTER ASSESSMENTS

Obviously, the present situation leaves much to be desired. What is the outlook for developing better methods of assessment? In light of the experience of scientists in other fields, and in view of the failure of psychologists to achieve concensus regarding personality variables on the basis of verbal definitions and human judgments, there is little reason to hope that improvements in assessment will result from continuing reliance on the human being as the essential component of assessment techniques. While human judges must continue, perhaps for a long time, to function in many applied settings, valiant efforts must be made to develop new and better techniques critically needed in both basic science and in the applied fields of psychology.

In spite of the complexity of the human personality and the correspondingly difficult task of developing firm knowledge of its structure and function, there are three reasons to believe that substantial progress will occur in the next few decades:

1. The availability of an increasingly large number of able and well trained professional persons supported by substantial research grants who are devoting their energies to basic research in the field.

2. A decrease in parochialism with respect to both theoretical orientation and methodology. Increasingly, it is being recognized that Construct X in Theory A may in fact be very similar to Construct Y in Theory B and that the important thing is not the perpetuation of one or the other but better assessments of each in order to determine their actual identity or uniqueness.

3. The availability of large computers makes feasible the design of experiments involving the parallel assessment of many variables by alternative methods and the analysis of the very large numbers of relationships among them.

But, neither sophisticated statistical techniques nor computers can accomplish anything except as a human being provides them with meaningful hypotheses *and* relevant data. It is clear, therefore, that human beings must play a number of critical roles in the developments ahead. While these several roles may be intertwined, they need not be, and it is therefore useful to discuss them separately. We shall consider the different functions of the human being, first, in the science of psychology, and then, in assessment practice.

THE ROLES OF THE ASSESSMENT PSYCHOLOGIST IN BASIC SCIENCE

AS AN OBSERVER

The basis of any science is the accumulation of a multitude of carefully recorded observations of relevant phenomena by sensitive human observers. Only on the basis of a very large body of systematically collected observations (raw data) can real progress be made with respect to the discovery of order in any domain. Although much assessment data has already been collected, much more and much better data must be collected to provide a solid basis both for the discovery of basic principles and for their sound application in practice.

AS A SYSTEMATIST

But observations alone, no matter how many nor how good they may be, do not provide the basis for ordering themselves into meaningful categories nor do they point to the dimensions on which they may be usefully compared. These are tasks that must be carried out by analytically minded scientists, whether they rely primarily on their own analytic skills to identify similarities and differences in recorded observations or on the extensive use of statistical techniques and electronic computers. The nature and value of any resulting taxonomy will depend greatly on the abilities, skills, and insights of the persons who undertake these essential tasks in the development of knowledge. Much progress has been made in developing better knowledge with respect to personality structure within the last 30 years, but a great deal of work yet remains to be done.

AS A PERSONALITY THEORIST

Scientists are not content merely with making observations and systematically ordering them into a structure. Immediately they begin to ask such questions as:

"What are the sources of the variations in the observed phenomena?"
"What attributes or dimensions or variables do these observations have in common?"
"What are the relationships among the attributes, dimensions or variables?"
"Why do such relationships occur—is there, perhaps, a common 'cause' for covarying phenomena?"

These and similar questions concerned with the identification of underlying variables and the relationships among them are the primary concern of personality theorists, who posit hypothetical constructs and develop hypotheses regarding relationships among them. Personality theorists may and often do suggest hypotheses regarding the most promising behavioral indicators of their hypothetical constructs. Theorizing in the domain of personality ranges all the way from loose speculation to relatively rigorous logical systems, but in all cases it can be done only by a human being. As in other fields of science, the relative merit of competing theoretical positions must be decided not by debate but on the basis of empirical evidence.

AS EXPERIMENTER

The verification or refutation of a theory—or more specifically the validation of the constructs and hypotheses which constitute a theory, is also the task of a human being—in the role of an experimental scientist. The theorist may, and often does, change hats and test his own ideas through experimentation, but to the extent that his constructs are clearly delineated and his hypotheses are explicit, the critical experimental tests of any theory can just as well be carried out by fellow psychologists.

In fact, it is the nature of science that what was a hypothesis becomes an accepted principle or "law" only if its predictions are supported by the results of independent experiments by other researchers.

The assessment psychologist as a basic scientist is interested in establishing the validity of the constructs used in personality theory and interested in establishing the construct validity of the operational measures used to assess these constructs. But only to the exent that such assessment measures can be shown to predict other behaviors in accordance with a theory can either the constructs or the measures of them be regarded as valid, and therefore, of potential utility in the field of practice.

THE ROLES OF THE ASSESSMENT PSYCHOLOGIST IN APPLIED SCIENCE

In the practical world, the assessment psychologist is usually faced with a situation requiring evaluations of individual persons as a basis for making one of several alternative decisions regarding them. A representative of some organization (a school, a hospital, an industry, or unit of government) asks his professional help in the practical day-to-day problems of assessing and making necessary personnel decisions regarding students, applicants, patients, or employees. From the standpoint both of the organization, and of the individuals involved, such decisions are always important, and sometimes critical. It is obviously desirable that the assessments be as good as possible so that the decisions based on them will be correct as often as possible.

Confronted with a request for professsional help in an applied setting, a psychologist has several options:

1. He may offer his services as an expert in the use of a particular technique which he believes enables him to arrive at generally valid assessments of persons. In doing so, he may limit his responsibility to describing persons, leaving to others the critical decisions to accept, hire, hospitalize, or promote. He may also accept the responsibility of recommending or making such decisions. A decision to use oneself and a preferred technique in a practical situation would most likely be chosen by professional persons relying primarily on considerable "faith validity" in their use of a specific technique.

2. The psychologist may state that the task proposed falls outside his field of expertness but suggest another person who could do the job. This response would suggest considerable faith validity in the assessments of a fellow psychologist.

3. The psychologist may reply that present knowledge and the "state of the art" are inadequate to be useful in contributing to a solution of the practical problems posed.

4. The psychologist may accept the challenge of the task but insist that his professional assistance will be of value only to the extent that he is permitted to function as an applied scientist responsible for (a) analyzing the problem in detail, (b) evaluating the efficacy of presently used procedures, (c) experimenting with new techniques, and (d) carrying on a continuing check of the validity of both old and new components of the program.

Available research evidence, as well as the personal experience of many assessment psychologists, suggests that of the above four alternatives, the last is the only appropriate choice open to responsible applied psychologists. Alternatives 1 and 2 are not acceptable because of the ever-mounting evidence regarding low reliabilities and validities of highly personalized assessments, especially when used to make the kinds of decisions required in the work-a-day world. Alternative 3 is not socially responsible; admittedly, the state of existing knowledge is woefully incomplete, but that which is known, plus the methodologies which are available, have regularly enabled psychologists to develop assessment programs in many different applied settings superior to the ones previously employed. In carrying out the undertaking as suggested in alternative 4 above, the applied psychologist, like his counterpart in basic science, must function in many roles.

IN DEFINING THE TASK

The organization requesting professional help in assessment has often not clearly analyzed the real problem confronting it. For example, an employer may complain about the low productivity of his employees and ask for help in selecting more productive ones when in fact the low productivity is a function of poor equipment, plant layout, or other conditions of work. An insurance company may believe that it wants to select its agents on the basis of the number of new policies sold, forgetting that its long-run profits are primarily a function of whether the policies sold by its agents are cancelled or continued. And, the staff of a mental hospital may think it wants assessments in terms of the traditional diagnostic categories of mental illness when, in fact, it needs prognostic assessments related to such decisions as the amount of freedom permitted each patient and the kind of treatment to which he is most likely to respond. The first task of an applied assessment psychologist, therefore, is that of working with other staff members of the organization to define the basic purpose(s) of the assessment program. Are assessments to be merely filed away or are they to be used to predict some future performance or in making decisions regarding people? If the latter is the case, what kinds of performance and what kinds of decisions? We shall again refer to this critical task in discussing the criterion problem below.

IN EVALUATING THE VALIDITY OF CURRENT PRACTICES

In moving into any new applied setting, the wise assessment psychologist begins by a thorough study of currently used procedures. This is desirable for two reasons. First, it gives him an excellent opportunity to learn a great deal about the organization and the thinking of those staff members with whom he must work closely in trying out new procedures. Equally important, it provides a necessary base line against which to evaluate the anticipated increment in validity resulting from modifications in the assessment program of the organization.

If he is fortunate, the psychologist may find that available records provide him with the necessary data to evaluate both the reliability and validity of each component of the existent program. More typically, he will find that the necessary data are simply not available. Therefore, he will have to develop systematic forms for recording both assessment data and performance (criterion) data of many kinds: interviewers' ratings, test scores, production records, supervisors' ratings, etc. Only then is he ready to proceed with a systematic evaluation of the strengths and weaknesses of the present system, identifying the sources of the low reliability and/or validity which resulted in the original request for his professional services.

IN DEVELOPING CRITERION MEASURES

One would suppose that any organization requesting professional help in assessment would be reasonably clear as to the nature of the criterion, i.e., the kind of performance against which alternative assessment techniques would be validated. Unfortunately, very little thought may have been given to the criterion. Often, there is a tendency for organizations to use the most convenient or readily available measure of performance, with little or no consideration of the possibility that alternate measures of performance (productivity, success, or improvement) might be more congruent with the basic goals of the organization.

The practical experience of psychologists has demonstrated that the assessment of criterion behavior is fully as complex as the assessment of traits and fraught with the same hazards. Suppose, for example, an employer is primarily interested in selecting employees for their productivity and relies on the judgments of a foreman to provide him with an index of productivity. Suppose, however, that these ratings of productivity are heavily colored by the foreman's personal liking for each employee. Under such conditions, it is clear that no assessment technique could possibly provide measures predictive of productivity since the criterion itself is not a valid index of productivity.

As a dramatic illustration of the problems associated with the development of suitable criterion measures, we again refer to the author's research on the selection of medical students (Kelly, 1957,

1963). The initial request was for assistance in selecting students who were capable of completing the requirements for the M.D. degree. The previously used (and most convenient) criterion measure was the grade record in medical school. When it was found that both first- and second-year grades were predicted more accurately by the overall premedical grade average than by the ratings of the members of the committee on admissions, the committee members were surprised, but defended their ratings on the basis of the fact that they were primarily concerned, not with predicting grades, but with predicting "competence as a physician." This, it was stated, would be reflected in the student's performance during the last two "clinical years" of medical school.

When it was discovered that their ratings did not predict judged performance in clinical courses as well as they had predicted first-year grades, it was decided that a search should be made for still additional measures related in one way or another to "being a good physician." Before the project was completed, a total of 54 possible criterion measures were obtained. In addition to grades, these included (1) sociometric ratings by the seniors of each other (e.g., if ten years from now you lived in a small community, who among your fellow students would you most prefer to have serve as physician to your own family?), (2) marks on the 14 State Board Examinations required for licensure, (3) scores on the six National Board Examinations, and (4) ratings on eight variables by the young physician's supervisor during his internship year in some hospital. While certain of these criterion measures correlated with each other closely, some did not correlate with any of the other 53! For certain variables, it was possible to determine that the lack of correlation was due to unreliability of the criterion measure itself. However, a factor analysis of these 54 criterion measures pointed clearly to at least five fairly independent dimensions of "success in medicine." And, although each of these five major criteria could be predicted with some validity, a different set of predictor variables (traits) was associated with each of them. (Incidentally, the ratings of the members of the committee on admissions were not the most useful in predicting any of them!)

This study has been described in some detail because it is becoming increasingly obvious that there are few if any situations in which a single measure or index of performance constitutes an adequate criterion. Thus, an employer who believes he wants to select his employees primarily on the basis of their productivity may discover, on further analysis, that because of the nature of the jobs in his factory, there is a high rate of turnover among highly productive employees; if so, it may turn out that the actual productivity of his operation will be increased by selecting employees who are willing to continue working at their jobs even though they are not as productive as those who resign after a few weeks of work. The moment one has identified two or more relatively independent criteria, predicted by different traits, one is confronted with the necessity of deciding how each of the criteria should be weighted in order to optimize some "super criterion," e.g., the long-range profitability of an industrial manufacturing operation. Since it is rarely, if ever, that one can obtain valid measures of such an ultimate or long-range criterion, decisions regarding the weights to be assigned to independent alternative criteria must be made, not by the assessment psychologist, but by the persons responsible for setting the goals of the organization. Thus the faculty of one medical school might properly decide to focus its efforts on the selection and education of general practitioners, another on those who will become medical scientists, another on those who will become leaders in the field of public health. All are equally laudable objectives, but the pattern of traits most likely to lead to success and satisfaction in one of these fields is simply not the same as that for others.

IN SPECIFYING PROMISING PREDICTOR TRAITS AND CHOOSING THE BEST TECHNIQUES FOR ASSESSING THEM

As soon as agreement has been achieved with respect to the criterion (or criteria) to be predicted and a suitable method developed for measuring it (them), the next tasks of the assessment psychologist are (1) analyzing the total situation in an effort to specify some sub-set of the hundreds of human traits which promise to be useful in predicting the criteria, and (2) selecting from among the large number of assessment techniques those most likely to yield reliable and valid measures of the traits specified. These represent critical steps, and their successful execution requires familiarity with the nature of the behaviors involved in the criterion performance, a broad basic knowledge of personality structure and functioning, and sound information regarding the strengths, weaknesses, limitations, and other essential characteristics of alternative techniques for assessing each of the traits specified. The eventual choice of specific techniques must be based not only on evidence regarding reliability and validity of the measures but also on other considerations such as their relative cost in both money and staff time and their acceptability to subjects. Typically, the psychologist ends up with a preliminary battery of techniques requiring much more time than would be acceptable for continued use; this is because he can be fairly sure that some of his hypotheses regarding critical traits and valid methods for assessing them will not be confirmed when put to the acid test of predicting criteria.

IN DETERMINING THE VALUE OF THE EXPERIMENTAL PROGRAM OF ASSESSMENT

The applied psychologist, like his counterpart in pure research, dares not accept the truth of his hunches, no matter how confident he may be that they are correct. Therefore, the applied psychologist must put a proposed program of assessment to an experimental test. Subjects (i.e., applicants, students, or patients) are assessed by the techniques chosen for trial, and the resulting measures (scores, ratings, etc.) are stored until criterion measures can be obtained for the same subjects.

Then, and only then, is the assessment psychologist in a position to evaluate the validity of each component of the assessment program. He computes the correlation of each variable with all other variables, both assessment and criterion measures. Using appropriate statistical techniques, he can quickly determine the optimal weighted combination of predictor variables (trait measures) for each criterion measure. At this point it is very common to discover that because many of the predictor variables are highly intercorrelated, an optimally weighted combination of a relatively small number of predictor variables will predict a criterion about as well as a larger number of them. If this proves to be true, it means that the assessment battery can be "pruned" to eliminate those techniques which yield only redundant information and hence do not increase the overall accuracy of prediction.

IN CROSS-VALIDATION AND FURTHER REFINEMENT

Assuming that the outcome of this long sequence of operations is reasonably successful, it might be supposed that the job of the applied assessment psychologist has been completed. This is not the case; even though the psychologist does not participate personally in the assessment process (as an interviewer, rater, or interpreter of any of the assessment data), there still remains one critical job for him—that of cross-validation. The statistical procedures used to assign optimal weights to predictor variables do so on the basis of the particular set of relationships among all variables *for the group of subjects used in the statistical analysis.* It is, therefore, essential that the entire operation be repeated for another group of subjects in order to estimate the validity of the selected set of predictor variables when used with other groups of subjects.

Even though the findings are replicated and hence can be trusted to be applicable to succeeding groups, it is still not likely that the assessment psychologist will have worked himself out of a job. Why? Primarily because the measured predictive validity of the best subset of trait measures for predicting the criterion is likely to be considerably less than desired either by him or the organization. The only assessment programs with "satisfactory levels of validity" are those which have not been subjected to an empirical test!

To the degree that greater accuracy of prediction is important to the organization, the psychologist may spend years of research in an effort to develop a still better assessment program. This time will be devoted to attempts to develop better criterion measures and to search for and check out the usefulness of trait measures which promise to increase the accuracy of predicting the criterion measures.

IN CONCLUSION

It is clear that the human being must and does play a very responsible and even a critical role in any sound program of assessment. Whether the immediate goal is (1) developing techniques for measuring hypothetical constructs and using them in testing hypotheses derived from a theory of personality or (2) assisting an organization in making more useful evaluations of, and hence wiser decisions about, the persons employed by or served by the organization, the tasks are remarkably similar. Both require a broad conception of the human personality, the ability to analyze a situation, a familiarity with a wide range of assessment techniques, the ability to formulate rigorous experimental tests of one's hypotheses, and considerable sophistication in psychometrics and statistics. In view of the complexity of the problem and the many demanding requirements of the total process of validation, it is easy to understand the tendency of so many individuals and organizations to rely on inadequate criteria of validity to justify the continued use of traditional techniques of assessment.

Improved methods of assessment will be developed, because they are critically needed both to achieve a better understanding of human personality and to improve the quality of decisions regarding individuals in society. But progress is likely to be gradual rather than dramatic. The problems of assessment are far too complex to expect simple solutions of them. An occasional breakthrough may be anticipated as with Binet's brilliant conceptualization of intelligence, not as the sum of a number of simple abilities (e.g., sensory acuities, speed of reaction, etc.) but as a complex mental capacity which develops throughout childhood and thus enables children to solve increasingly complex problems as they mature. This concept in turn led to the developmental concept of mental age. And, since children were found to develop at different rates, Stern proposed that the ratio of mental age to chronological age be used as an index of the rate of intellectual development and this was the origin of the concept of the intelligence quotient or IQ. While none of these conceptualizations of intelligence has resolved all of the issues involved, each contributed greatly to improving the quality of assessments of intellectual ability.

No one has yet come up with equally promising conceptions of important noncognitive dimensions of human functions, and methods of assessing them. Although everyone agrees regarding the importance of traits such as emotional maturity, social adjustment, and individual responsibility, thus far there is no real consensus regarding their definition and measurement. However, enough different psychologists are sufficiently convinced of the reality of a basic and important continuum underlying these presently diverse labels to justify a belief in an early breakthrough with respect to its assessment. Loevinger, in a recent paper (1966), suggests that these and related conceptions of development may be eventually coalesced and assessed as "ego development."

In view of the tremendous complexity and the infinite varieties of human beings, there will always remain much grist for the mills of poets and prophets. Lest the reader be concerned that the development of improved methods of assessment will serve to reduce the challenge of dealing with the most complex of all living organisms, it must be remembered that each discovery in any field of science only serves to increase the boundaries of the unknown. While the precise measurement of general intelligence may properly be regarded as a major achievement of psychology, and while measures of general intelligence are extremely useful in a variety of practical situations, further research on the nature of intelligence has indicated that there are many different kinds of intelligence. Assessing each of the several varieties of intelligence and discovering the relationship of each to other personality traits represents a continuing challenge. Breakthroughs leading to improved assessment of other important human characteristics will inevitably contribute to a better understanding of personality and be of great value in the world of practical affairs.

REFERENCES

Allport, G. W., Vernon, P. E., and Lindsay, D. B. *A study of values.* Boston: Houghton-Mifflin, 1960.

Allport, G. W., and Odbert, H. S. Trait names: A psycho-lexical study. *Psychol. Monogr.*, *47*, Whole No. 211.

Anastasia, Ann. *Differential psychology—individual and group differences in behavior*, 3rd ed. New York: Macmillan, 1958.

Applezweig, D. W. Some determinants of behavioral rigidity. *J. abnorm. soc. Psychol.*, 1954, *49*, 224–228.

Blum, G. S. *Psychodynamics: The science of unconscious mental forces.* Belmont, Calif.: Brooks/Cole, 1966.

——————. *Psychoanalytic theories of personality.* N. Y.: McGraw-Hill, 1953.

Buros, O. K. *Tests in print: A comprehensive bibliography of tests for use in education, psychology, and industry.* Highland Park, N. J.: Gryphon Press, 1961.

——————. *Mental measurements yearbook*, 6th ed. Highland Park, N. J.: Gryphon Press, 1965.

Cattell, R. B. *Personality and motivation—structure and measurement.* Yonkers, N. Y.: World Book, 1957.

Coombs, Clyde. *A theory of data.* New York: Wiley, 1963.

Cronbach, L. R. Test "reliability;" its meaning and determination. *Psychometrika*, 1947, *12*, 1–16.

——————. The two disciplines of scientific psychology. *Amer. Psychol.*, 1957, *12*, 671–684.

——————. *Essentials of psychological testing.* New York: Harper, 1960.

Cronbach, L. R., and Gleser, Goldine. *Psychological tests and personnel decisions.* Urbana: Univ. of Illinois Press, 1965.

Dreger, R. M., and Miller, K. S. Comparative psychological studies of Negroes and whites in the United States. *Psychol. Bull.*, 1960, 57, 361–403.

Edwards, A. L. *Edwards personal preference schedule.* New York: Psychological Corp., 1954.

Forer, B. R. The fallacy of personal validation: A classroom demonstration of gullibility. *J. abnorm. soc. Psychol.*, 1949, *44*, 118–123.

Fuller, J. L., and Thompson, W. R. *Behavior genetics.* New York: Wiley, 1960.

Galton, Francis. *Hereditary genius.* New York: Appleton-Century-Crofts, 1870, and Horizon Press, 1952.

Goldberg, L., and Werts, C. E. The reliability of clinicians' judgments—a multi-trait, multi-method approach. *J. consult. Psychol.*, 1966, *30*, 199–206.

Gough, H. G., and Heilbrun, A. B. *The adjective check list manual.* Palo Alto, Calif.: Consulting Psychologists Press, 1965.

Guilford, J. P. *Personality.* New York: McGraw-Hill, 1959.

Hays, W. L. *Quantification in psychology.* Belmont, Calif.: Brooks/Cole, 1967a.

——————. *Basic statistics.* Belmont, Calif.: Brooks/Cole, 1967b.

Kelly, E. L. Alternate criteria in medical education and their correlates. Proceedings of the 1963 Invitational Conference in Testing Problems, Princeton: Educational Testing Service, 64–85.

——————. Multiple criteria of medical education and their implications for selection. *J. med. Educ.*, 1957, Part II, 185–198.

——————, and Fiske, D. W. *The prediction of performance in clinical psychology.* Ann Arbor: University of Michigan Press, 1951.

Kretschmer, E. *Physique and character.* London: Routledge and Kegan, 1925.

Landis, C. Questionnaires and the study of personality. *J. nerv. mental disease*, 1936, *83*, 125–134.

Loevinger, Jane. The meaning and measurement of ego development. *Amer. Psychologist*, 1966, *21*, 195–206.

McClellan, D. C., Atkinson, J. W., Clark, R. A., and Lowell, E. L. *The achievement motive.* New York: Appleton-Century-Crofts, 1953.

Malcolm, E. A study of the validity of individual personality profiles based on each of four projective techniques. Unpublished Ph.D. dissertation, Univ. of Michigan, 1952. See *Diss. Abstr.*, 1952, *12*, 221.

Mead, Margaret. *Male and female, a study of the sexes in a changing world.* New York: Morrow, 1948.

Meehl, P. E. *Statistical vs. clinical predictions.* Minneapolis: Univ. of Minnesota Press, 1954.

Murray, H. A. *Explorations in personality.* New York: Oxford Univ. Press, 1938.

O.S.S. Staff. *Assessment of men.* New York: Holt, 1948.

Remmers, H. H., and Elliott, D. N. *The Purdue rating scale for instruction.* West Lafayette, Ind.: Univ. Book Store, 1960.

Sawyer, Jack. Measurement and prediction, clinical and statistical. *Psychol. Bull.*, 1966, *66*, 178–200.

Sheldon, W. H., and Stevens, S. S. *The varieties of temperament.* New York: Harper, 1942.

Strong, E. K. *Vocational interests of men and women.* Stanford, Calif.: Stanford Univ. Press, 1943.

Taft, R. The ability to judge people. *Psychol. Bull.*, 1950, *52*, 1–23.

Taylor, Janet A. The relationship of anxiety to the conditioned eyelid response. *J. exp. Psychol.*, 1951, *41*, 81–92.

Tyler, Leona E. *The psychology of human differences.* New York: Appleton-Century-Crofts, 1956.

——————. *Tests and measurements.* Englewood Cliffs, N. J.: Prentice-Hall, 1966.

Ulrich, L., and Trumbo, D. The selection interview since 1949. *Psychol. Bull.,* 1965, *63,* 100–116.

Vandenberg, S. D. Contributions of twin research to psychology. *Psychol. Bull.,* 1966, *66,* 327–352.

Vernon, P. E. Some characteristics of the good judge of personality. *J. soc. Psychol.,* 1933, *4,* 42–57.

——————. *Personality assessment: A critical survey.* London: Methuen, and New York: Wiley, 1964.

Wenger, M. A. Studies in autonomic balance in Army Air Forces personnel. *Comp. Psychol. Monogr.,* 1948, *19,* No. 101.

NAME INDEX

Allport, G. W., 2, 29, 103
Anastasia, Ann, 5, 103
Applezweig, D. W., 33, 103
Atkinson, J. W., 46, 104
Bender, Loretta, 57
Blum, G. S., 14, 29, 89, 103
Buros, O. K., 79, 103
Cattell, J. Mck., 88
Cattell, R. B., 26, 103
Clark, R. A., 104
Coombs, C., 27, 103
Cronbach, L. R., 37, 86, 88, 103
Dreger, R. M., 4, 103
Edwards, A. L., 29, 46, 103
Elliott, D. N., 64, 104
Fiske, D. W., 57, 84, 104
Forer, B. R., 85, 103
Freud, S., 88, 90
Fuller, J. L., 4, 103
Galton, F., 3, 4, 88, 103
Gleser, Goldine, 86, 103
Goldberg, L., 84, 103
Gough, H. G., 104
Guilford, J. P., 15, 67, 104
Hathaway, S. R., 30
Hays, W. L., 3, 20, 32, 44, 104
Heilbrun, A. B., 104
Hippocrates, 13
James, W., 14
Jung, C. G., 14, 15
Kelly, E. L., 31, 57, 78, 80, 84, 96, 104
Kelvin, Lord, 87
Kretschmer, E., 13, 14, 55, 104

Landis, C., 60, 104
Leacock, S., 23
Lindsay, D. B., 29, 103
Loevinger, Jane, 101, 104
Lowell, E. L., 104
McClellan, D. C., 46, 104
McKinley, J. C., 30
Malcolm, E., 84, 104
Mead, Margaret, 4, 104
Meehl, P. E., 70, 74, 104
Miller, K. S., 4, 103
Mira, L. R., 57
Murray, H. A., 46, 104
Odbert, H. S., 2, 103
Pearson, K., 3
Plato, 2
Remmers, H. H., 64, 104
Rorschach, H., 27
Sawyer, J., 22, 74, 75, 104
Sheldon, W. H., 14, 55, 104
Spranger, E., 29
Stevens, S. S., 104
Strong, E. K., 31, 104
Taft, R., 67, 103
Taylor, Janet, 89, 104
Thompson, W. R., 4, 103
Trumbo, D., 75, 105
Tyler, Leona, 104, 105
Ulrich, L., 75, 105
Vandenberg, S. D., 4, 105
Vernon, P. E., 1, 2, 29, 103, 105
Wenger, M. A., 55, 105
Werts, C. E., 84, 103

SUBJECT INDEX